Representing Time in Natural Language

Representing Time in Natural Language

The Dynamic Interpretation of Tense and Aspect

Alice G. B. ter Meulen

A Bradford Book
The MIT Press
Cambridge, Massachusetts
London, England

© 1995 Massachusetts Institute of Technology

All rights reserved. No part of this book may be reproduced in any form by any electronic or mechanical means (including photocopying, recording, or information storage and retrieval) without permission in writing from the publisher.

This book was set in Palatino by Asco Trade Typesetting Ltd., Hong Kong and was printed and bound in the United States of America.

Library of Congress Cataloging-in-Publication Data

Meulen, Alice G. B. ter.
Representing time in natural language : the dynamic interpretation of tense and aspect / Alice G. B. ter Meulen.
    p.   cm.
"A Bradford book."
Includes bibliographical references and index.
ISBN 0-262-20099-6
1. Grammar, Comparative and general—Temporal constructions.
2. Grammar, Comparative and general—Verb. 3. Space and time in language. I. Title.
P294.5.M48   1995
415—dc20   94-23917
                                                                      CIP

voor Hein, in memoriam

Contents

Preface

The expression of the aspect is the expression of a way of taking (hence, of a way-of-dealing-with, of a technique); but used as a description of state.
Ludwig Wittgenstein

We learn what language is, not just by studying it as an abstract system, but also by looking closely at how we use it to convey information. Insights resulting from such studies may help us formulate assumptions and hypotheses about our cognitive capacities to understand language. Mathematical models simulating how we describe change in the world and express the passage of time in natural language provide a window on our cognitive capacities to reason with partial information about what happened. This book presents a systematic investigation of how we use the temporal information given in texts or discourse to reason in time about the flow of time. The tools of semantic representation employed in this book are to an important extent inspired by some fundamental assumptions and logical techniques developed in Situation Semantics by Barwise and Perry (1983). Their account of dynamic interpretation and the central notion of situated inference incorporates context as an essential ingredient in the computation of meaning and informative content. Besides the more often studied accumulation of information on a fixed, static, or stable world, within a logical space of its alternatives and possible variations, the subject examined here is the dynamic process of interpretation and the preservation of temporal information in a continuously changing world.

This book is the result of purely theoretical investigations. No experimental or observational studies were conducted with actual speakers of a language, nor were computers programmed to emulate human reasoning about the flow of time. Cognitive scientists who consider such tasks to be part of their enterprise may want to make use of the insights, predictions, or representational tools developed in this book. The results of this theoretical research are certainly claimed to have empirical significance, and hence explanatory and predictive power within the generative linguistic research program of universal grammar. Even though the linguistic data in this book are limited to English, and no comparative data have been considered, the interpretive principles and semantic constraints formulated here should prove to find expression in all natural languages. The abstract semantic principles governing tense and aspect constrain the set of possible natural languages considerably, demarcating them from the logically possible ones as those communicative systems that exploit their relation to the constantly changing external world efficiently.

This book has taken either two months or more than ten years to write, depending on whether the progressive *writing a book* is interpreted strictly or liberally, allowing for possibly extended intermissions in the writing. The seeds for the views developed here were contained in a chapter on the compositionality of aspectual classes within Montague Grammar, part of my dissertation (ter Meulen, 1980). That chapter has guided my subsequent research program on the dynamic interpretation of tense and aspect. The rapid developments in the 1980s in dynamic model-theoretic semantics for natural languages, when Situation Semantics and Discourse Representation Theory took over from "classical" static Montague Semantics, provided a wealth of new tools, puzzles, and explanatory insights. The issues and questions a semantic theory of tense and aspect had to address changed radically in a dynamic account of informative flow and the incremental interpretation of discourse. My choice to design a representational system suitable for reasoning about time in natural language has been motivated in part by the existing wealth of descriptive semantic insights on tense and aspect, contrasting with the relatively poor understanding of valid reasoning patterns, and my intention to seek contentful linguistic applications of situated inferences. Because we must express our reasoning *about* time *in* time, our language contains the means to indicate what changes and what does not, relative to where we are and how we are changing. Studying the interaction between such dynamic and static information provides central insights into the perspectival properties of information, which make natural language such an efficient and environmentally conscious tool of communication.

The first opportunity to work on this project was provided by a postdoctoral appointment from 1981 to 1984 at the University of Groningen, The Netherlands, at the invitation of Johan van Benthem. This book finally delivers on a long-standing promise I then made to him to write a book single-handedly. Over the years I have profited a great deal from discussions on natural-language semantics and logical-linguistic theory with numerous Dutch colleagues, of whom I can only explicitly mention here Renate Bartsch (who carefully read the entire manuscript and provided numerous comments), Martin Stokhof, and Jeroen Groenendijk, Theo Janssen, Co Vet, Pim Levelt, Sjaak de Mey, Frans Zwarts, Eric Reuland,

Jack Hoeksema, Marina Nespor, Paul Dekker, Frank Veltman, Michael Moortgat, Henk Verkuyl, and Henk Zeevat. I gratefully acknowledge the sabbatical year 1992–1993 from Indiana University, which enabled me to complete this project at the Institute for Logic, Language, and Computation of the University of Amsterdam.

I learned to appreciate how the interaction of current syntactic theory with semantic theory could benefit both when I joined the Department of Linguistics at the University of Washington in 1984. Discussions with Joe Emonds on aspect were always insightful, talking to Ellen Kaisse made me first realize that graphs would make my views more accessible, and Fritz Newmeyer rightly urged me to be cautious with claims about causatives. Since 1989 Indiana University has provided me with a stimulating environment for this research in the IU Logic Group and its Cognitive Science Program. I am most indebted to Jon Barwise for designing Situation Theory to model the flow of information and situated inference, which has proven to be an essential toolkit for linguistic applications, as pursued in this book. Larry Moss patiently volunteered his time for on-the-spot assistance when the toolkit did not seem to fit my intentions easily. Jerry Seligman's collaboration on the formalization of the notion of chronoscopes and the dynamic aspect trees (DATs) has been crucial in clarifying some logical aspects of such graphical representations as inference tools.

There are many people to whom I am otherwise indebted for help, long-distance collegial support, and invaluable critical comments. For many years now Hans Kamp has been showing me what the study of meaning is really all about. His continued support, stimulating influence, even when our views seemed to diverge, and his unfaltering optimism about my ever forthcoming book on a topic to which most significant contributions are his, have been essential to me. The dynamic interpretation developed in this book departs from some of the crucial insights of Kamp's Discourse Representation Theory, but ultimately shares more foundational assumptions of the underlying theory of meaning and interpretation than the apparent differences in toolkits would seem to suggest.

Barbara Hall Partee was the first to point out the deep parallels between nominal and temporal quantification that kept intriguing me. On numerous occasions she has provided the right next questions, corrections, or new puzzles to make me think further. Her work on temporal anaphora and quantification has guided me in seeking to model situated reasoning about time in DATs, although our resulting explanations differ importantly.

To the Generic Research Group, consisting of Jeff Pelletier, Greg Carlson, Gennaro Chierchia, Godehard Link, and Manfred Krifka, I owe a good deal of gratitude for letting me experiment with linguistic applications of Situation Theory in a relatively protected environment, during the Linguistic Summer Institute at Stanford University in 1987 and at several of our later meetings. Chapter 4 in this book is most obviously indebted to the collective research results of this group (published in Carlson and Pelletier 1994).

To Nancy Cartwright I am indebted for ineffable support and for characterizing capacities in nature in such a way that they can play their causal role in the background of this dynamic semantics.

Aravind Joshi, Harry Stanton, Teri Mendelsohn, and the editorial staff at the MIT Press have been extraordinarily patient during the temporally extended production of this book. The anonymous readers' reports have helped me significantly to clarify some issues and elaborate on the specific advantages of DAT representations during the last stages of revision. My former student Steve Ryner assisted me expertly with the graphics, saving me from investing more of my time in laborious drawings.

Zeno Swijtink kept facilitating our "complete life" in adverse circumstances, however single-minded and incomplete I must at times have been when writing this book. Timen and Joris rightly insisted that if the book was to be any good, it should at least have pictures.

I dedicate this book to the memory of my brother Hein, for he used to admonish me that time is created by our actions.

Chapter 1
Introduction

Competent speakers of a natural language share an essential cognitive capacity to describe change in their world as consisting of certain events that took place and states that were the case. On the basis of what we explicitly assert as having happened, we automatically make all kinds of inferences about what must have happened when. Some of these inferences arise because we attribute causal structure to parts of the described episode. Other inferences are triggered by word meaning, world knowledge, personal prejudice, presumptions, or private information. If semantic theory is intended to contribute to our understanding of the human cognitive endowment, it must address the general question of how the given information is used in such reasoning about temporal relations in natural language.

1.1 What Are Aspectual Classes?

When we describe what has happened, we face a host of linguistic choices in constructing an informative narrative about it. Obviously, however small a part of our past we wish to describe, many different things happened at the same time, and others occurred in a definite temporal order. Yet we must give information about it in strict linear order, sentence by sentence. How do we sort and classify the continuously changing world into different events and convey in what temporal order these took place? For most ordinary communicative purposes it is too simplistic a narrative style to describe everything in the order in which it happened (though very young children tend to do this in their "this-and-then-and-then" stories). Lots of things may have happened simultaneously; and some things may have lasted for quite some time whereas others changed instantaneously. Ordinarily, the linear order in which we are bound to express our information does not reflect the temporal order in which the described changes actually occurred. Well-crafted stories do not give such a play-by-play account of what happened. Quite freely jumping back and forth in time, as it were, we encode the information about what happened in an informative, coherent, and useful description, relying on our cognitive abilities to reason about their temporal relations. In certain specific contexts, the order we give our utterances in discourse does mirror the temporal relations between the events described. But in other contexts, the order of description is entirely independent of the temporal order of what is described. How then does the recipient of such information reconstruct, at least up to a certain extent, what happened when? How is information about the temporal relations extracted from what we say, when it is not explicitly asserted?

Obviously, the choice of verbal tense and aspect matters a great deal in descriptions of what happened. This book focuses on the simple past tense, the perfect, the progressive, and only certain uses of the present tense, studying their interaction in detail.[1] But tenses only partly indicate in which order the described events took place. Sometimes a sequence of pure simple past tenses without any temporal adverbials does mirror the temporal order in which the described events happened, as in (1.1).

(1.1)   A car hit the fence. The driver was killed. The police arrived.

We immediately infer from (1.1) that the car hit the fence *before* the driver was killed and that the police arrived *after* the car had hit the fence. Anyone who understands (1.1) does not need to give it much thought to realize that these are the right temporal relations. Temporal adverbials like *before, after, while, when, since,* and *until* explicitly describe such temporal relations between situations.[2] We often reason using such adverbials in our conclusions, even when the given information did not contain any.

In other contexts, however, a sequence of three simple past tense sentences (that is, sentences whose verbs are in the simple past tense) does not reflect the temporal order. An illustration is given in (1.2).

(1.2)   Jane was so happy. She sang, danced, and clapped her hands.

For (1.2), a natural interpretation, though by no means the only possible one, is to think of everything as happening simultaneously: Jane was happy, clapped her hands, danced, and sang, all at the same time. If competent users of a language have no trouble deciding which temporal relations hold given certain descriptive information, then cognitive processes must underlie this fundamental capacity, which causes the differences in the interpretation of (1.1) and (1.2). Such processes should be characterized by a logical theory of meaning and interpretation, if it is to model our temporal reasoning in natural language. It should explain in a sufficiently general way how conclusions about the temporal relations between parts of a described episode are derived from the information given about it.

Clearly, prior context may predispose an interpreter to understand a sequence of simple past tenses as reflecting the order in which things happened. In (1.3), for instance, the context created by the first sentence forces the second one, identical to the second sentence of (1.2), to describe events that did *not* take place at the same time.

    (1.3)   Jane did three things consecutively. She sang, danced, and clapped her hands.

The second sentence is now understood as describing three sequential events. Because context so obviously matters to interpretation, the semantic rules should characterize how a sentence used in different contexts expresses different temporal information. This requirement forms the foundation of our study of situated temporal inference.

From these first observations we may conclude that tenses put some constraints, however weak, on how the described events are related in time. The simple past tense itself merely requires that what is described happened before the information about it was given. Aspect contributes crucial information about the temporal architecture of the descriptive information. The observed difference between (1.1) and (1.2) is caused by a fundamental difference in the aspectual class of the descriptive information, which determines to an important extent how information we get later is related to the events we already have information about.

Knowledge of the world and its causal connections may also play an important role in determining how the described events are related in time. A clear example of this is (1.4), based on common knowledge of the physical relation between dropping a glass and its breaking.[3]

    (1.4)   The glass broke. Jane dropped it.

If we interpret the second simple past tense sentence in (1.4) as describing an event that caused the event described in the first sentence, it explains why the glass broke. Since causes precede their effects, the sequence in (1.4) reverses the order in which the events it describes happened.[4] When such causal connections are used as additional constraints in the interpretation, we may understand a sequence of two simple pasts as describing events that happened in the reverse order, overruling the temporal relations determined by aspectual information. But a semantic theory for natural languages should not have to venture into the realm of physics or commonsense knowledge about causal structure. In this book temporal reasoning is considered a form of logical reasoning, in which quantificational force, binding, and context change are core concepts. The much broader, more ambitious enterprise of analyzing what other sources of information we may use in arriving at certain conclusions about what happened when is part of the domain of artificial intelligence and knowledge representation in cognitive science. It is crucial, therefore, that semantic theory determine what options may be left open by the information given, so that other modules of information may provide additional constraints that the central logic "service" of the system may exploit in generating conclusions.

Often the interpreter of a text has a certain amount of choice about whether to understand a subsequent sentence as describing an event following the event described by the previous sentence. The meaning of the verb or its arguments may partially determine the choice, and knowledge of the world may contribute additional constraints.

> (1.5)   Jane felt ill. She sat down, attempted to decipher the
>   message, and looked at her watch. She sighed. It was not
>   even noon yet.

From (1.5) we infer quickly that Jane felt ill *before* noon and looked at her watch *after* sitting down and *while* feeling ill. But it is less clear whether her attempt to decipher the message temporally included her looking at her watch or whether that attempt ended before she looked at her watch. In the first case we would infer that she looked at her watch *while* she was still attempting to decipher the message. In the second case she looked at her watch and sighed, *no longer* attempting to decipher the message. Both interpretations leave it entirely open whether she ever succeeded in deciphering the message, though both are perfectly determinate in inferring that it all happened before noon and while she was feeling ill. Such interpretive choices are pervasive in natural-language texts as well as in other media for efficient communication. It is not the task of semantic theory to prescribe what interpretive choices should be made in such cases, or which choice is the best, the "most natural," or even the preferred one in a given case. Semantic theory should characterize in what contexts such interpretive options arise and what the semantic consequences are of taking any of the open options. The account of temporal reference and reasoning presented in this book therefore regards interpretation as an indeterministic process, but characterizes the semantically determinate consequences of interpretive options in its conditional constraints on content. Other domains of knowledge or information may be adduced to constrain the open options further, but such more general accounts of reasoning are beyond the intended scope of this book. Any theory of temporal reasoning in natural language must contain a core of logical inferences using tense and aspectual information, which may well be context-dependent and situated, as explained later.

Part of what we do in constructing an interpretation is to decide on such options. If we choose to interpret a following tensed clause as describing a following event, we commit ourselves to certain consequences. For example, if we interpret the second sentence of (1.5) to mean that Jane's looking at her watch made her stop deciphering the message, we must interpret the next sentence *She sighed* as describing an event occurring after she stopped.

If we impute such a causal correlation to her looking at her watch and stopping her attempt to decipher the message, her sighing cannot possibly be a temporal part of her attempt to decipher the message. But if that sentence had been in a perfect tense instead (*She had sighed*), we would have been free to infer that her sighing occurred during her attempt to decipher the message, even if we adhered to the causal correlation. If no causal correlation is intended and we interpret her looking at her watch as occurring while she was deciphering the message, her sighing can be interpreted as also being simultaneous with it.

Making such interpretive decisions depends on the aspectual class we assign to the clause. The classification of inflected clauses into aspectual classes contributes essential information about the temporal relations between the events and states described by a narrative text. This determines the temporal architecture of the representation of the descriptive information about what happened. Other factors may induce additional interpretive constraints, including causal correlations, prior context, background assumptions, prejudices, presuppositions, and the thematic roles of verbal arguments.

1.2 Controlling the Flow of Information: Filters, Plugs, and Holes

We have already seen that there are some important semantic differences between the use we make of the simple past and the use we make of the perfect in temporal reasoning. Let us examine these differences further. The simple past *Jane sighed* in (1.5) describes an event of Jane sighing that must have occurred before this information was given. We do not know exactly when, for how long, or how many times she sighed. We do know that her sighing lasted a while and took place after she sat down. Since her sighing has now ended, she must now be in the state of *having sighed*. The perfect *Jane has sighed* describes this state caused by the end of her sighing. Such perfect states are atemporal in the sense that once they have begun, they never end. Perfect states themselves do not participate in the changing world of causal forces. Although a causal explanation may very well appeal to such a perfect state as a background condition, it does not describe such states as the causal source of change. The information expressed in the perfect tense, that Jane has sighed, admits only the inference that she sighed some time ago; it does not determine when she sighed. Reported with a perfect clause, her sighing could have taken place before, or after, or while she sat down. But with a simple past the context gives certain clues about how her sighing is temporally related to the other described events. In this case we also infer that she has sighed, but now we have at least some partial information about when the sighing took place, using the position of the clause in the narrative text.

It is very hard to detect any difference between the simple past and the perfect by looking at sentences in isolation. But ordinarily information is given to us embedded in a context, containing at least the very act of issuing that information, its surrounding situation, the old information, and a host of background assumptions and other interpretive constraints. When interpretation is viewed dynamically as the process of determining the content of a sentence dependent upon its context, the semantic differences between past and perfect tense show up in how we reason with such information about the temporal relations between the described events. The difference between the simple past and the perfect is hence aspectual in nature: the former describes events in a context-dependent way, whereas the latter gives only stative information.

The aspectual classes and aspectual properties assigned in the interpretation of a discourse determine how the events in the described episode are temporally related. Aspect controls the dynamics of the flow of information about described change encoded in a text. It plays a central role in determining what the descriptive information is about. Besides stative information, to which we return below, three means of dynamic "flow control" are distinguished to correspond to the three traditional aspectual classes of events.[5] Although natural languages differ considerably in how these three aspectual classes are expressed and lexicalized, they must all encode them somehow. Aspect is hence part of our universal linguistic capacity to classify and describe the world around us, just as tense is. The semantic characterization of the aspectual classes should not be tied to a language-particular lexicalization or argument structure.[6] Although the focus of this book is limited mostly to English examples, it would constitute a very interesting project to study in more detail how the semantic representations designed here are applied to the different ways aspectual classes are encoded in the rich variety of natural languages.[7]

Three modes of aspectual control are recognized in the system of dynamic interpretation presented here: *holes, filters,* and *plugs.* In the traditional terminology of aspectual classes *holes* correspond to activities or processes, descriptions of events that apply throughout their internal structure homogeneously (typically using verb phrases like *drive around, hover above, pour, damage*). *Filters* correspond to accomplishments (also, confusingly, called "events" in the literature), which are descriptions of change that never apply to any part of an event they describe (typically using verb phrases like *walk a mile, drive home, land, package, destroy, die*). *Plugs* are special cases of filters, commonly called "achievements," which are in a conceptual sense instantaneous, since they do not consist of an initial and a final stage (typically using verb phrases like *arrive, finish, begin, start*).

Aspectual information regulates the flow of the descriptive information and determines what it refers to. Besides aspectual and descriptive information, linguistic expressions ordinarily contain perspectival information, relating the source of the information to what is being described, sometimes captured as "point of view." The role of perspectival information is further analyzed in chapter 5, but first the representation of descriptive and aspectual information must be addressed. The contribution of holes, filters, and plugs to the architecture of the representation, regulating the flow of descriptive information, is characterized abstractly as follows.[8]

If we interpret a given clause describing an event as a *hole*, then we interpret the information expressed in the next sentence of the text as describing of a temporal part of that event, as if the information it conveys flows through the hole.[9] The context created by representing an event as a hole incorporates new information as describing an event temporally included in the hole.

If we interpret a given clause describing an event as a *filter*, then it restricts the information that flows through it to describing whatever else happened simultaneously. No part of a filter may be of the same type as the filter itself, so the clause interpreted as a filter refers to the smallest event of that type in that context. Filters create a choice between interpreting the next clause as describing a later event and interpreting it as describing an event temporally included in the filter.[10] If the first option is taken, subsequent clauses in the simple past tense must be interpreted as describing events occurring after the filter as well. In such an interpretation either the information about what else happened during the event represented as a filter may be reported later by using a perfect, or the perspective must be refined to make the internal parts of the filter accessible, as explained in chapter 5.

If we interpret a given clause describing an event as a *plug*, then it blocks all information about whatever happened at the same time. No new information can flow through it, so to speak, so it forces the context to redirect its temporal focus, interpreting the next sentence as describing another, later event. A plug represents the smallest event in the given perspective, so constrained that none of its internal structure is accessible for description. Further information cannot serve to discriminate the temporal parts of a plug, unless the perspective is refined. In this sense plugs are descriptions of atomic events, minimal relative to the given perspective. The perspective may change in the course of an interpretation and be refined later in order to discriminate more internal structure in events once considered atomic (see section 5.2).

This initial characterization of aspectual classes in terms of holes, filters, and plugs that control the flow of descriptive information and determine the architecture of the representation is perhaps somewhat metaphorical at first sight. Its formalization in dynamic aspect trees (DATs) and chronoscopes is presented in chapter 3, capturing these essential intuitions about the flow of information in precise definitions and logical concepts to account for reasoning with partial information about time.

Natural languages contain diverse linguistic means to encode the description of change as holes, filters, or plugs. In English the clauses in (1.6) are simple examples of sentences that are ordinarily, disregarding special contexts, interpreted as holes.

(1.6)   a.   Water spread over the floor.
        b.   I bought clothes.
        c.   Mary walked along the river.
        d.   John damaged his car.

Events described as holes typically end rather than finish, since the descriptive information about them does not indicate how they get completed. Such events last for some time and endure throughout the periods described by durative adverbial modification (e.g., *for an hour, three hours long*). In English, indefinite mass NPs (1.6a) or bare plural arguments of the verb (1.6b) virtually enforce the interpretation of the clause as a hole in any context, since they typically allow the description of the entire event to be equally applicable to any of its parts. For example, if (1.6a) describes a past event of water spreading over the floor that ended before this information was given, there must be a smaller event contained within it that is also a past event of water spreading over that floor. Prepositional phrases like *along the river* in (1.6c) that do not describe a definite measure or container, but rather a path or a continuous change of location, may be used in descriptions of events as holes (see Jackendoff 1991). Some lexical verbs such as *damage* in (1.6d) or *patrol* also allow the part-whole inference characteristic of holes. If a given clause is interpreted as describing a hole, its starting point must precede the event described by any subsequent simple past tense clause, though states, described with perfect tenses, may temporally overlap with it. However, causal connections or other knowledge of the world can interfere with and overrule these general semantic principles determining temporal dependencies. As we saw in section 1.2, a clause may be interpreted as describing an event before the event described by an earlier clause, if it describes a causal or explanatory connection to its cause.

Filters put a fairly weak constraint on the flow of information. A clause interpreted as a filter gives information about the smallest event of the type representing its descriptive content. When an event is represented as a filter, further information may describe either what else was going on at the same time or an event later than the one the filter refers to. (1.7) gives simple examples of English sentences that are typically interpreted as filters, momentarily disregarding the influence of context and background.

(1.7) a. The book fell on the floor.
       b. I bought a book.
       c. I drank a glass of water.
       d. Mary walked to the river.
       e. John destroyed his car.

Filters are descriptions of the kind of event that may finish or get finished, and that does not merely cease or end. They have traditionally been conceived as goal-directed or "telic," indicating what would constitute their completion, although that notion is notoriously hard to make precise. What, for instance, completes my buying of a book? The transfer of cash from the book's buyer to its seller is only one way to complete a sale; there are hosts of other ways, some of which, like electronic bank-transfers, are temporally and physically rather removed from what actually goes on in the store. Why would buying a book be completed, whereas buying poetry, interpreted as a hole, presumably merely ends when one stops buying more poetry? Another much-cherished example of such a telic event or accomplishment is the complex action of climbing a mountain. Although there seems to be some intuitive inclination to consider such climbing completed when the top of the mountain is reached, any experienced mountaineer would be hard pressed not to include in his successful climbing of a given mountain the often much more demanding descent. His return to safety at his point of departure would constitute successful completion of the mountain-climbing act. Pressure to give substance to this intuition of the completion of an event described as a filter, as opposed to an end of an event described as a hole, quickly leads into the murky waters of counterfactual reasoning, causation, and inferences with *ceteris paribus* clauses.[11] These equally rely on descriptions of events as filters and hence do not offer much help. Instead of relying on completions, for semantic purposes we need only acknowledge that filters are descriptions of smallest events of the given type that allow, but do not require, further information to be interpreted as describing later events. Filters are descriptions of events with singular count or amount-term arguments, modified by goal-describing PPs (e.g., (1.7a,d)) or container-adverbials (e.g., *in an hour, within a day*). Such modification does not require that the event lasted throughout the hour or the day, but expresses only that the event took place inside the specified period. Of course, if (1.7b) describes a smallest event of the buying of a book, it is fixed which book is bought. I could well have bought some other books along with it. I could even have bought one of those other books within the time it took for me to buy the first one. But I could not have bought that first book within the time that I bought it, for I would then have bought the same book twice. If this sounds trivially true, consider why it is that one does not simultaneously drink water twice, even though within the time it takes to drink some specific quantity of water, one also must drink another, smaller quantity of water. Similarly, why is it that one destroys a car only once, but can damage it often, repetitively or gradually? Holes do not describe such smallest events of the given type; only filters do.

This core semantic difference between holes and filters cannot be captured merely in terms of the truth-conditional content of propositions, understood as static functions from situations or worlds to truth-values. It is not that the syntactic expression *I bought a book* cannot be true of a subevent of the given event it is true of. If I buy several books simultaneously, I may well buy a book while buying another one. But it must be *another* book that I buy simultaneously. An existentially quantified proposition does not keep track of which book is being referred to; hence, the sentence *I bought a book* is true of two different objects—in other words, true twice over in the intended situation.[12] Modeling of temporal reasoning requires fixing in the context all that is indeterminate in the descriptive information encoded in the type. Hence, the event of my buying this particular book, while simultaneously buying that other one, is distinguished from my buying the same book twice, which must be temporally distinguished events of buying that book.[13]

The start of an event described as a filter precedes the start of any event described by subsequent clauses, but the end of the event described as a filter is preceded by the end of any described part of it. In that sense, filters serve as semantic objects incorporating information about the (partly) simultaneous subevents. This allows us to infer from the two filter descriptions *Jane climbed Mont Blanc. She walked up to the base camp* that her starting to climb Mont Blanc must have preceded her starting to walk up to the base camp and that the end of that walk to the camp must have preceded the end of the climb. (Such inferences are further analyzed in chapter 2.) Holes give us similar precedence information about their starting points, but they do not give us any direct information about the temporal relations between their endings. So from *Jane drank some water. She ate some chips*, we infer that she must have started eating chips after she had started drinking water, but we cannot be sure whether her eating her last chip preceded her drinking her last bit of water.

If we describe what happened as a plug, no further information can describe its temporal parts, unless the perspective of the description is refined. Plugs do not let any information about their subevents through, relative to the given perspective. The internal structure of an event described as a plug is rendered inaccessible to further description. Their finish is not distinguishable in the representation from their start, despite the commonsense knowledge that even such "atomic" events do take time. Because their beginning cannot be distinguished from their ending, they are in a semantic sense "instantaneous" transitions. Linguistic examples of plugs often depend more strongly on context than examples of holes and filters. Lexical meaning plays a more important role in plugs, which often use verbs describing change that cause stative background conditions for the descriptions of events. The examples in (1.8) are often used as illustrations of plugs in English.

(1.8) a. Jane arrived.
       b. The bomb exploded.
       c. I won the race.
       d. The lecture started.
       e. The winner finished in five minutes.

Descriptions of transitions between temporary states are often plugs. For example, (1.8a) and (1.8b) describe the causal transition between the state of Jane's not being here and the state of her being here, and between the original state and the resulting one caused by the explosion. Descriptions of beginnings (i.e., transitions from negative polarity in a type to its positive) or endings (i.e., transitions from positive polarity to its negative) are natural examples of plugs, as in (1.8d, e). The aspectual verbs *start* and *finish* themselves describe plugs, instantaneous switches between off-on-states. In chapter 2 such aspectual verbs are formalized as special transitions, so-called polarity flips. But the aspectual verbs *keep* and *continue*, describing continuations, clearly describe holes and admit durative adverbial modification. Performative uses of verbs like *promise* or *request* in first person present tense make good examples of plugs, but only in truly performative contexts. They have a very special self-referential semantic characteristic of describing their own content. They cannot fail to be true, if certain characteristic "felicity conditions" are met. Interpreted as performatives, of course, they induce constraints on future actions, plans, and goals of the participants. When plugs are modified by temporal inclusion adverbials, as in (1.8e), the adverbial characteristically describes a period ending with the plug. Sometimes this period also contains a presupposed event or the given event, representing the content of the clause last processed. For example, (1.8e) means that it took the winner five minutes to win, not that the finish itself lasted five minutes, so the presupposed start and the described finish are both included in the five-minute period. But if (1.8d) were so modified, it would mean that five minutes elapsed between the event last described and the start of the lecture, since *start* does not carry any such presuppositions (see chapter 2).

Aspect is concerned with the way we represent change in the world as structured transitions. We use aspectual information to organize descriptive information about the world, so aspectual properties are not determined by what is the case in the world. Events are in the world, but nothing about their physical structure makes them plugs, filters, or holes. We create holes, plugs, and filters to classify the reference of our descriptions, to communicate efficiently about them, and to make our descriptive information hook up properly to the changing world. A plug is a semantic ticket to disregard change internal to the described event, to treat it as atomic and close off its internal structure to further description. Of course, later we may reconsider and come back to the event, unplug it to unveil more of its internal structure. We then treat it as a filter that lets new information through about what else happened simultaneously. Such perspectival refinement is discussed in more depth in chapter 5.

1.3 Situated Reasoning about Time

Reasoning with a text uses its informative content, expressing descriptive, aspectual, and perspectival information while preserving its supposed truth, and draws conclusions that express further information about the same described episode or part of it. The information obtained from interpreting the text must include the information expressed in the conclusion. The text and the conclusion describe different events belonging to the same episode.[14] The text contributes the information as an ordered set of premises of the argument, constructing a context in which the conclusion must be true as well, if the argument is valid. Reasoning is understood here as a heterogeneous cognitive action relating elements of at least five domains:

1. information obtained by interpreting a text or discourse,
2. common knowledge, presuppositions, and background assumptions,
3. the external world,
4. someone performing the reasoning, and
5. personal information, prejudices, and preferences.

A logical analysis of reasoning must characterize this truth-preserving manipulation of information describing parts of the world as a formal and algorithmic procedure. In any natural context, we reason and make inferences based on partial and often very limited information about what is or was the case. Complete information about even a strictly demarcated subject matter is a goal we may strive for, but in actual exchanges of information never do attain. In natural language we manipulate information very efficiently, gaining further information from what we are given and what we assume to be true (even if only for the sake of argument), and resorting to more global or coarser description whenever the given information is more detailed than it needs to be. Our linguistic and cognitive capacities to synthesize information and express it in natural language are a fundamental but embarrassingly little understood aspect of our human cognitive endowment. This inherent partialness of information in our linguistic descriptions and the flexibility of descriptional grain should be considered virtues rather than vices of our communicating in natural language. They are in fact essential for the tremendous efficiency of natural language as a carrier of information. It would be a misconception of the flexibility of natural language to assume that a semantic theory of natural language could exhaustively list all the logically possible interpretations of a given expression in all its possible contexts of use. Since speakers can always supply more information, other contexts, or more details upon request, the interpretation of natural language in context is always open to representational refinement and inherently indeterministic.

To give these general semantic concepts of information, reasoning, and inference more precise content, we need a systematic way to represent the information contained in an English text. The dynamic semantic interpretation in DATs, presented in chapter 3, formulates rules to construct such representations of information obtained by processing English texts and characterizes conditions based on such representations to reason about the temporal relations between events described in the text. In such temporal reasoning the order in which the information is given often matters a great deal. The text does not just give us an unstructured lump of information, but a structured object in which a temporal vantage point is fixed from which the available information is surveyed. This temporally located vantage point is the primary factor that makes temporal reasoning *situated:* whether the conclusion is validly inferred from the given information depends on "where you are" after interpreting the premises. As a consequence, some information that was given using a simple past tense may later have to be reported in a conclusion using a perfect verbal inflection instead. Similarly, when we receive information that something is going on, later we may have to infer that it must have ended, when certain other information is given to us. But, of course, there are ways of giving information so that it is never affected by subsequent changes in context. Natural language contains a variety of means to indicate whether the information given is or is not affected by subsequent changes in context.

In interpreting a text about the past, using either past perfect, past progressive, or simple past inflections, the event of uttering the clause or otherwise issuing the information is always located after the events described. The source of the information is an event that terminates the past. When the verbal inflection is present perfect, the source is a temporal part of the perfect state that began after the past event causing this state ended. This dependence on the event of uttering or issuing the information contributes a secondary factor to situated reasoning about time. It is a different dependence than the primary one, because it does not contribute directly to the control of the information flow about the described events. This dependence is perspectival in creating a relation between the source and the changing temporal vantage point of the interpretation. Perspectival information is the third kind of information supplied by the interpretation of a text, besides the descriptive and aspectual information discussed above. Perspectival shift is triggered by aspectual properties, and perspectival refinement is an operation restructuring the representation also controlled by aspectual properties of the interpreted text.

In the study of temporal reasoning as a form of situated inference, temporal adverbials describing temporal relations between situations obviously constitute core data. We have already seen examples in section 1.1. Even when the premises are not connected by temporal adverbials, the conclusion may contain such adverbials explicitly describing the temporal relations between the situations described in the given information. The adverbs *while, when, before, after, since, until, now,* and *then* are all interpreted as describing relations between situations. Interesting further examples of inferences from (1.1) and (1.2) are given in (1.9) and (1.10), respectively. (* indicates invalid inference.)

(1.9)   a.   The car hit the fence before the driver was killed.
         b.   *The car hit the fence when/after the driver was killed.
         c.   The driver was killed when/after the car had hit the fence.
         d.   The car had hit the fence before/when the driver was killed.
         e.   *The driver had been killed after/while the car hit the fence.
         f.   The police arrived after the driver was killed.
         g.   The police arrived when the driver was dead.
         h.   The police arrived when the car had hit the fence.
         i.   The car having hit the fence, the police arrived.

(1.10)   a.   Jane danced while clapping her hands.
         b.   Jane was happy when/while she danced.
         c.   While Jane was dancing, she was happy.
         d.   *While Jane was happy, she was dancing.

The interaction between perfect and simple past descriptions is another important issue in temporal reasoning.[15] We see in (1.9c–e) that *after, before,* and *when* describe temporal relations between perfect states and events, but the described state must have held already before the described event started. If the perfect is used in describing what happened, the event causing the perfect state is entailed. Such entailments may need to be represented explicitly by accommodation, a form of updating the available information that should never affect the current perspective. Events described by simple past tense clauses and interpreted as filters and plugs do affect the perspective by shifting the temporal vantage point, as we will see in the next chapters.

However, the order of occurrence of a perfect clause in the text or sequence of clauses does give us some temporal information. Consider a text consisting of three clauses: a simple past tense clause, followed by a past perfect tense clause, followed by another simple past tense clause. The event that caused the perfect state must precede both the event described by the preceding simple past tense clause and the start of the event described by second simple past tense clause. A slight modification of (1.1), shown in (1.11), illustrates this effect.

(1.11)   The car hit the fence. The driver had been killed. The police arrived.

From (1.11) we validly infer (1.12).

(1.12)   The driver was killed before his car hit the fence and before the police arrived.

But if the perfect clause occurs as the last one in a sequence of three tensed clauses, as in (1.13), we could not validly infer (1.12).

(1.13)   The car hit the fence. The police arrived. The driver had been killed.

Intuitively, (1.13) may well be used to describe a case where the police killed the driver in chasing him, but not necessarily before his car hit the fence.

Inferences with *since, until,* and *when* show an interesting interaction with progressive clauses and aspectual verbs such as *start, continue, keep, resume, end,* and *finish.* For example, from the simple past tense premise in (1.14a), the valid inferences in (1.14b–e) can be drawn.

(1.14)   a.   The bomb explosion ended my lecture.
         b.   Since the bomb exploded I have not continued lecturing.
         c.   I was lecturing until the bomb exploded.
         d.   My lecture was not finished when the bomb exploded.
         e.   I did not keep lecturing when the bomb exploded.

The inferences in (1.14) make central use of aspectual verbs, the topic of chapter 2. It is clear that the intrinsic semantic relations between aspectual verbs and the aspectual classes need to be spelled out in detail in a proper account of temporal reasoning. Observe that in (1.14b) and (1.14c) *since* and *until* describe a temporal relation between one event and the starting point or the end point of the another state or filter event. Their semantic properties appear to be interestingly different from those of *after, before,* and *when,* but I will not pursue this topic here, since temporal adverbials and their interaction with aspectual classes lie outside the scope of this book.

Inferences with *now* and *then* are even more revealing of the essentially situated character of temporal reasoning. The few simple examples in (1.15) make it clear that the changes in a context affected by the dynamic interpretation of a text allow such deictic adverbials to shift their reference accordingly and do not depend merely upon the source issuing the information.

(1.15) a. Jane left the station. She was now ready to call. She saw a phone booth, and was taking money out of her wallet. Then she found the note again.
   b. Now the bomb has exploded, I wonder whether my lecture is over. At the emergency training, I was not told what to do then.

From (1.15a) we infer that Jane was ready to call *when* she had left the station, and that she found the note *while* taking money out of her wallet. From (1.15b) we infer that I started wondering *after* the bomb exploded and that *then* refers to the generic case of bomb explosions, not to this particular explosion. The indexicals *now* and *then* appear to be much more flexible in anaphorically referring to situations in the context, other than the source, than has been considered in the philosophical treatments of demonstratives.[16]

As a final point in this introductory chapter, we need to clarify what a context is or what is considered "given," when a new clause is interpreted. A context is conceived of quite broadly in this book. It includes at least the following five components:

1. lexicon + syntax of the language,
2. situated and logical inference rules,
3. other semantic constraints,
4. the available information, and
5. elements of the situation of use.

The lexicon determines the meaning of the descriptive vocabulary of the language. It also fixes the referents of names for objects, including individuals, substances, and kinds. The exact form of lexical entries is presented in detail in section 6.1 in connection with their syntax. Other semantic constraints may be used to determine what information is expressed by a clause in a text. An important function performed by such constraints is the representation of the presuppositions of a clause, conditions that must be satisfied in a given context for the new information to be incorporated into it. Such presuppositions play an important anaphoric role in the semantics for aspectual verbs, developed in chapter 2. Some semantic constraints may be quite global in nature, but some may be local to the subject matter or domain described and may even depend on particular matters of fact in the situation described.

The available information is, of course, quite a mixed bag. It includes the information obtained by processing the prior text or discourse, determining the "temporal point of view" at which the interpretation is continued or inferences are made. The aspectual classes have the special role of determining whether new information describes the same event or another one, temporally distinguished from it. Hence, the available information is not just a set of facts or static representations of information that is assumed to be true. Instead, it is a highly structured component of the context that contributes essential constraints to the continued interpretation of the linguistic input. New information may sometimes merely increment the given information without affecting any part of it. But often new information requires that the representation of the given information be modified. Temporal information sometimes requires introducing new events and resetting the given temporal vantage point to the one last introduced. Such changes of context are triggered by certain sequences of tensed clauses, as we have already seen. If such a context change is triggered, it affects how the remaining given information should be reported as conclusions in inferences. The rules that govern such changes in context can be made quite explicit and precise, and that is exactly what this book is intended to do. A particularly interesting form of temporal context change is perspectival refinement, when a plug is unplugged to incorporate information about its temporal parts. This requires that part of the represented information is momentarily "subtracted"—as it were, put on hold—and the temporal point of view is traced back under specific constraints to an event described by prior linguistic input. Such perspectival refinement has important structural consequences for the representation of given information. Chapter 5 presents this formal notion of a perspective, ways of changing it, and perspectival coherence in more detail.

When we reason with given information, we assume that it is true, but that assumption may prove to be unwarranted in part at a later point in the interpretation. What can we do with false information? It is unwise to use it in making inferences, for the conclusions obtained from it may not be true. Perhaps it can give us information about its source, as being unreliable or not well informed. False statements are still descriptive of something, supposedly, since their content is not void and they do have meaning. But a false statement does not describe anything in the world; it cannot hook up to something that really happened. Negative (as opposed to false) information describes what is not actually the case. It can be used in reasoning and can be hooked up to the real world in part. Little attention is devoted in what follows to what we do when the assumption that given information is true turns out to be unwarranted. But the interpretation of negative information is certainly of interest to a general theory of temporal reasoning with partial information.[17]

Chapter 2
The Aspectual Verbs

English has lexicalized aspectual verbs that describe the internal temporal structure of events: their onset (e.g., *start, begin, commence, initiate, resume*), their middle (e.g., *continue* and *keep*), and their end (e.g., *end, finish, terminate, halt, cease, complete*). In this chapter the logical properties of these aspectual verbs are analyzed. The way we use such aspectual verbs in inferences and temporal reasoning exhibits their logical meaning and determines their interaction with various forms of negation and their relations to the aspectual classes controlling the flow of information. The results constitute the basis for the dynamic representation of temporal information in DATs in the next chapter.

2.1 The Linguistic Data

When an event starts, no stage of it has yet occurred, although other events of the same type (i.e., with the same participants doing the same thing) may have occurred earlier. But when an event continues, resumes, stops, ends, or finishes, part of it has already occurred, for at least it must have started. Such an assumption about what must already be included in the available information is a *presupposition*, a constraint on what the context must contain for the interpretation to proceed. Of course, when we interpret *Jane continued to read this book*, we do not just assume that one or another arbitrary initial stage of Jane's reading of this book has occurred. But the starting stage that is presupposed must be the onset of this particular reading that she now continues to do. She may well have been reading this book in the past and even have finished reading it then. But all such stages are temporal constituents of other past events of her reading this book, temporally preceding the one being described as continuing now. The presupposition is hence not merely existential, but essentially anaphoric in character. It is the onset of *this* event of her reading this book that must have occurred already, not merely some beginning of some event of the same type. In other words, no ending or finishing stage of this event has yet occurred. Such anaphoric presuppositions play an important role in how we use information in reasoning about temporal relations between described events.

A well-known characteristic of presuppositions is that both positive clauses and their negative counterparts require the same presupposed information. This is illustrated in (2.1), where (2.1a–d), when uttered with no special intonation or contrastive stress, all presuppose the same perfect tense clause in (2.1e).

(2.1) a. Jane stopped reading this book.
       b. Jane did not stop reading this book.
       c. Jane continued reading this book.
       d. Jane did not continue to read this book.
       e. Jane had started reading this book.

Note that the simple past of the aspectual verbs in (2.1a–d) presupposes past perfect clauses containing the information about the beginning of the event. The starting stages that caused these perfect states preceded the stage described now as (not) stopping or (not) continuing. We infer that the context contains such first stages, because the stative information of their presuppositions entails that they occurred before. Updating a context with presupposed or entailed information does not affect the current temporal reference, determining which event is being described by new information.

The fact that only the aspectual verbs that describe the onset of an event carry no presuppositions is related to their acceptability with expletive subjects in English, as in (2.2).

(2.2) a. There started a lecture on anaphora.
       b. *There finished/continued/resumed a lecture on anaphora.

These facts attest to the indefiniteness of the aspectual verbs that describe the onset of events. As (2.3) shows, extraposition of NPs from their internal subject position as in (2.2a) is restricted to such indefinite, presupposition-free aspectual verbs.[1]

(2.3) a. A lecture started on anaphora.
       b. *A lecture continued/finished/resumed on anaphora.

The aspectual verbs that describe the onset of an event are regarded as having existential force in the dynamic interpretation, introducing a first stage of the described type of event in the context. They describe the action of turning the event on (i.e., a transition terminating its off-state and starting an on-state of the same type).

Just as the universal quantifier in predicate logic is definable as the external negation of the existential quantifier with an internal negation, *continue/keep V-ing* is equivalent to *not start not V-ing*, preserving throughout the presupposition *have started V-ing*.[2,3] So *keep* and *continue* have quantificational force, preserving the given on- or off-state of the event-type, whichever it happens to be. Pursuing this heuristic analogy with predicate logic, we see that the internally negated existential aspectual verb *start not V-ing* is lexicalized in English by verbs describing the suspension, ending, or completion of the event (e.g., *finish, terminate, complete, halt, stop, end, cease*). We will return to the semantic differences between these verbs, after looking more closely at the quantificational force of the continuation verbs.

If the event being described is ongoing and not interrupted, the same information is given by using either *keep* or *continue*. However, one striking difference in how we use *continue* and *keep* lies in their presuppositions. *Keep V-ing* requires that the action is actually going on. For instance, you cannot *keep* reading unless you are reading at this very moment. But if you *continue* to read this book after a break, you may resume reading and then presumably keep reading. So *continue to V* does not require that one is actually *V-ing*, since it allows the event to be resumed first, if it was interrupted. This is evident also in (2.4), when a story is reported in several installments.

(2.4)   This story is to be continued/*to be kept (on).

Using *continue* therefore induces a more liberal constraint on the internal structure of the event that is continued, allowing as it were the interrupted bits and pieces of it to be collected into one single event. Within such a discontinuous, gappy, or scattered event there still is one unique start and one unique finish or end, but possibly many stops, interruptions, and corresponding resumptions.

The different semantic properties of these quantificational aspectual verbs are apparent also in imperatives of stative verbs.[4]

(2.5)   a.   Keep quiet!
        b.   *Continue to be quiet!
        c.   Be quiet!

Using (2.5a) presupposes that the addressee is already quiet and asks her to stay that way. Of course, one may also very effectively use (2.5a) in a situation where the addressee is obviously not quiet and force her to accommodate the presupposition. Using the stative imperative (2.5c) does not carry that presupposition, but orders the addressee to become quiet, if she is not. In part, the unacceptability of (2.5b) is accounted for by the fact that infinitival reports of simple states like *to be quiet* cannot be used as complements of aspectual verbs, as observed in chapter 1. A much more important reason, however, is that states cannot be resumed, since they lack the internal temporal structure characteristic of events. What (2.5b) would express is expressed in the simple imperative (2.5c).

Now that we have identified both existential and quantificational aspectual verbs, the issue arises whether the unselective binding of indefinites by quantifiers familiar from Discourse Representation Theory (DRT) research is also observed with quantificational aspectual verbs.[5] The answer is indeed positive, but it requires some further understanding of the aspectual classes to which these aspectual verbs themselves belong and the temporal anaphora they create. Observe first that the quantificational aspectual verbs *keep/continue* take durative adverbial modification and accordingly behave like holes, letting further information through that describes their parts.

(2.6)   Jane kept dialing for half an hour. No one answered.

From (2.6) follows (2.7), which makes the universal force of *keep* explicit.

(2.7)   Every time Jane dialed (within that half hour), no one answered.

Each dialing is hence a temporal antecedent for a not-answering. Contrast this with the existential aspectual verb in (2.8a).

(2.8)   a.   Jane started dialing. No one answered.
          b.   When Jane dialed, no one answered.

The existential *start* leads to an inference about just that one time Jane dialed. Of course, the general rules of temporal anaphora apply here too in (2.8). Jane's starting dialing takes place before the not-answering, because the aspectual class of *start* classifies it as a plug. Note that the aspectual class of the complement of a quantificational aspectual verb does not affect the temporal anaphora; the anaphora is affected solely by the aspectual verb in (2.9).

(2.9)   a.   Jane started to read. She saw a mouse.
          b.   Jane kept arriving late. She left on time, but the traffic was horrendous.

Reading is classified as a hole, but in (2.9a) Jane's seeing the mouse is not a temporal part of her starting to read, though it may still be simultaneous with her reading and certainly is simultaneous with her having started reading. So *start V* is a plug, irrespective of the aspectual class of the main verb. If *arrive late* is classified as a plug, the same unselective binding is observed in (2.9b) as in (2.6) and (2.7). The binding of *keep/continue* is unselective, since several complements may be coordinated, all of which are simultaneously bound. But if an indefinite singular count NP is an internal argument of the verb, represented by a type with a free new parameter, it escapes from this aspectual binding and still remains available for binding pronouns in subsequent clauses, according to the accessibility conditions of DRT.[6] These two facts are illustrated in (2.10).

(2.10) a. Jane kept reading and writing.
        b. Jane kept reading a book. It was about tense and aspect.

If we want to use *keep* or *continue* to describe an event that follows an event just described, either we must first explicitly assert that this event ended or was finished, or our descriptive information must be incompatible with its continuing. This incompatibility may, for instance, be caused by the two types having inconsistent sets of entailments. For example, the text in (2.6) can be continued in two ways, with (2.11a) and (2.11b).

(2.6)   Jane kept dialing for half an hour. No one answered.

(2.11) a. She stopped dialing and looked around.
        b. She left the phone booth.

The continuation in (2.11a) explicitly describes Jane's dialing action as now stopping, and since *stop* is a plug, it precedes her looking around. The continuation in (2.11b) entails that she is no longer dialing, accommodating the presupposition that she had been using a phone located in a phone booth. Incompatibility of entailments triggers an update of the context that restructures the representation of the given information in such a way that the event described next is also interpreted as occurring later. This updating process is elaborated in chapters 3 and 5.

If quantificational aspectual verbs are represented as holes, no matter what the aspectual class of their complement, their binding domain is not limited to sentential boundaries, as is ordinarily the case for universal NPs or universally quantifying adverbials.[7] The generalization that NP arguments in the nuclear scope of a quantifier do not bind pronouns across sentential boundaries does have a parallel in the semantics of aspectual verbs: the complement of a quantificational aspectual verb is rendered "inaccessible" as antecedent for later events. But with existential aspectual verbs the complement describes an event temporally preceding the event described by the next sentence, as observed in (2.9a). Only the entire *keep* clause, or the maximal V projection, serves as temporal antecedent for descriptions of events that occur later. This explains why we infer (2.12a) directly from (2.6) followed by (2.11b). But in order to infer (2.12b) from this, we must appeal to the principle that any temporal part of an event e that precedes another event e' precedes e too.

(2.12) a. She had been dialing for half an hour before she left the phone booth.
        b. No one had answered when she left the phone booth.

Finally we should consider the semantic properties of the verbs that describe the ending of events. Remember from chapter 2 that only filters may be finished, whereas holes are ended, unless their temporal boundaries are somehow determined beforehand in the context.

(2.13)   Jane finished *driving around/driving home.

One can end something before finishing it, but not finish it before ending it, as is obvious in (2.14).[8]

(2.14)   a.   They ended the meeting agreeing to finish another time.
          b.   *They finished the meeting agreeing to end another time.

Another semantic difference between *end* and *finish* that plays a role in later chapters is the constraint on individual-denoting internal arguments with *end*, such as (2.15a–b).

(2.15)   a.   She finished the call/the apple.
          b.   She ended the call/*the apple.

Though an event can only be finished or ended once, it can be stopped or halted many times and resumed later. All verbs of ending require that what is going on not be continued any longer after the described action; that is, the action is turned off. But they differ in their ability to individuate an event: only *finish* and *stop* describe plugs that mark the transition between the event itself and the perfect state of its having occurred; *end* merely indicates that there was no resumption after the event was last stopped, which is negative and hence stative information.

Three more specific facts about the complementation properties of aspectual verbs deserve note here. First, *cease* is the only verb in the terminal class that admits infinitival complements (2.16a). Second, only *keep* requires an overt verbal complement and lacks any transitive use with an internal argument (2.16b). Third, in contrast, only *end* cannot take a verbal gerund or infinitival complement, but in its transitive use requires an event-denoting internal argument (2.16c).

(2.16)   a.   cease reading/to read
          b.   keep *a book/reading a book
          c.   end his reading/*reading his book

These lexical differences in argument structure need a proper explanation, but the logical behavior of these verbs requires us to analyze first their relation to the various forms of negation.

2.2 Negation and Duality: The Basic Tools

Starting to read describes the action that turns a state of not reading into a state of reading, and *stopping reading* describes the reverse action, turning the ongoing reading off. Such a semantic relation between predicates is called a *contrary* relation, relating all pairs of aspectual verbs listed in (2.17) as on/off switches of the polarity in their complement.

(2.17)   start/stop, start/finish, stop/resume, resume/finish,
             keep/end, continue/end

To represent these relations in such a way that their contrariness is explicit, we first need to design our representational toolkit. This system is to encode in DATs how information about the flow of time is extracted in the process of interpreting discourse or narrative texts.

Events are what the flow of time consists of: the basic constituents of our constantly changing world. In the representational system being designed here, events are not taken as primitives; instead, they consist of relations, objects related by them, and either a positive $(+)$ or a negative $(-)$ polarity. All kinds of things enter into relations: you and I, chunks of matter, abstract entities, scattered objects—indeed, whatever is describable as related to other things, including events and relations themselves. In order to capture what an event consists of, types are formed that classify events into similarity classes based on their constituent parts. One and the same event can be classified as belonging to or "being of" many different types, since we can describe one part of the world as constituting different kinds of changes. One and the same type can classify many distinguished events as constituting a similar kind of change occurring at different times. These concepts were first introduced informally in chapter 1, but the time has come to formalize them.

Boldface italic R, R', R'', or R'' or boldface italic counterparts of English expressions represent such relations, and boldface italic a, b, c, ..., a_n or boldface italic counterparts of names represent such objects that are related. Types are formed by putting a relation, objects, and a positive or negative polarity inside double angled brackets, representing that a relation holds or does not hold between particular objects. Two examples are given in (2.18).

(2.18)   a.   «*R*, *a*, *jane*, $+$»
            b.   «*read*, *jane*, *representing time*, $-$»

(2.18a) reads as "Relation R positively relates object *a* to Jane" and (2.18b) as "The relation of reading does not relate Jane to *Representing Time*." The exact correspondence between English expressions and these types is of course a major issue, deferred to chapter 6 where a fragment of English with a dynamic interpretation is specified. In natural language different clauses may be used to express the same information; by contrast, in different contexts the same clause may convey different information. For the moment, it suffices to understand that (2.18b), for example, could well represent part of the information obtained by interpreting my utterance last night of *His sister-in-law didn't read it*.

Besides these objects, relations, and polarities, types may also contain indeterminate objects or *parameters*, holding a place, as it were, for determinate objects. For the moment, think of these intuitively as blank areas on a map. They may carry information on how whatever is in that area relates to other things represented on the map, but we have no information about just what it consists of. In chapter 7 more philosophical issues are addressed about how these parameters should be regarded in semantic theory and why we manage to use them successfully in referring to the external world. To represent parameters, standing for objects or for relations and mixing freely with them, simple italic is used in the types (see R and R'' in (2.19)); x, y, z, x_n are included among the parameters for objects standing in relations.

(2.19)   a.   «$R, a, x, +$»
        b.   «$R'', x_3, y, -$»

Note that the polarities are always determinate constituents of types and have no corresponding parameters.

When a situation is correctly classified by a certain type with a positive polarity, the relation and objects in the type match the constituents of the situation.[9] When a situation is correctly classified by a certain type with a negative polarity, the relation does not hold between the objects in the type representing the constituents of the event. In either case we say the situation *supports* the type and represent this support relation by the symbol $\models$ as in (2.20a). When a situation does not match the constituents of the type, it does not support the type, for which we use the symbol $\not\models$, as in (2.20b).

(2.20)   a. $s \models$ «$R, a, b, +$»
        b. $s \not\models$ «$R, a, b, +$»

The interaction between the positive and negative polarity of types and the support relation is defined in (2.21), where for notational simplicity a type with a positive polarity is abbreviated as T^+ and one with a negative polarity is abbreviated as T^-.

(2.21)   If $s \models T^+$, then $s \not\models T^-$

For instance, taking for T^+ the type «*Read, jane, +*», (2.21) expresses that if Jane is reading in situation s, then it is not also the case that she is not reading in s. Thus, if a positive type T^+ is supported in s, then its negative counterpart T^- cannot be supported in s. Or with contraposition: if a negative type T^- is supported in s, then s does not support its positive counterpart T^+. Note that the other direction of the conditional in (2.21) is not generally defensible. A situation that does not support Jane's reading may simply not contain Jane as a constituent; hence, it can support neither the positive nor the negative type of Jane's reading. If it cannot be verified whether Jane is reading, it cannot be concluded either that she is reading or that she is not reading.

When types contain parameters, they are called *parametric types* or *parameterized types*. Using a positive parametric type to classify a situation tells us that some, not further specified part of that situation stands in the relation to the other constituents in that type. In principle, it must always be possible to describe that situation more fully and specify what it is that stands in the relation. Writing $T^+(x_1,\ldots,x_n)$ for the positive parametric type T in which the parameters $x_1,\ldots,x_n$ occur, its support is defined in (2.22).

(2.22) a. $s \models T^+(x_1,\ldots,x_n)$ iff
              s contains some objects $a_1,\ldots,a_n$, $s \models T^+(a_1,\ldots,a_n)$
         b. $s \not\models T^+(x_1,\ldots,x_n)$ iff
              s contains no objects $a_1,\ldots,a_n$, $s \models T^+(a_1,\ldots,a_n)$

When a parametric type correctly classifies a situation, that situation must contain an object with which it supports its nonparametric counterpart, filling the blank areas on the map, as it were. Not supporting a parametric type in a situation amounts to the negation of the positive clause. Any situation that does support it must be outside the current situation; in other words, positive evidence that the type is supported must be elsewhere. Supporting negative parametric types is even more tricky, since negation interacts with the aspectual classes, sometimes acting as a constraint over the entire current situation. The support of basic negative parametric types is defined in (2.23).[10]

(2.23) a. $s \models T^-(x_1,\ldots,x_n)$ iff
              every $a_1,\ldots,a_n$ in s, $s \models T^-(a_1,\ldots,a_n)$
         b. $s \not\models T^-(x_1,\ldots,x_n)$ iff
              some $a_1,\ldots,a_n$ in s, $s \not\models T^-(a_1,\ldots,a_n)$

Clause (2.23a) requires that the corresponding negative nonparametric type be supported throughout the situation supporting the negative parametric type. For example, when someone is not reading in a situation, nowhere in that situation is she reading. Not supporting a negative parametric type requires that there be some objects in the situation that fail to support the negative type. There is a gap somewhere in the situation where the interpreter does not get any information about the type one way or another. Such local lack of positive or negative information makes the support of the negative parametric type break down.

Now checking the conditional in (2.21) gives (2.24).

(2.24)   If some objects $a_1, \ldots, a_n$ in s, $s \models T^+(a_1, \ldots, a_n)$, then some $a_1, \ldots, a_n$ in s, $s \not\models T^-(a_1, \ldots, a_n)$

The existential aspectual verbs describe actions that flip the polarity of the type encoding the descriptive information expressed in their complement. When you start to read, you stop your not-reading state. When you stop reading, you start a not-reading state. These observations are captured in (2.25) as relations between supported types, with an intended interpretation of constraints over the DATs, as characterized in chapter 4.

(2.25)   a. $\forall s\ [s \models$ «*STOP*, «$R, x_1, \ldots, x_n$, $+$», $+$» $\Leftrightarrow$
          $s \models$ «*START*, «$R, x_1, \ldots, x_n$, $-$», $+$»]

   b. $\forall s\ [s \models$ «*FINISH*, «$R, x_1, \ldots, x_n$, $+$», $+$» $\Leftrightarrow$
          $s \models$ «*START*, «$R, x_1, \ldots, x_n$, $-$», $+$»]

   c. $\forall s\ [s \models$ «*STOP*, «$R, x_1, \ldots, x_n$, $+$», $+$» $\Leftrightarrow$
          $s \models$ «*RESUME*, «$R, x_1, \ldots, x_n$, $-$», $+$»]

   d. $\forall s\ [s \models$ «*END*, «$R, x_1, \ldots, x_n$, $+$», $+$» $\Leftrightarrow$
          $s \models$ «*KEEP*, «$R, x_1, \ldots, x_n$, $-$», $+$»]

   e. $\forall s\ [s \models$ «*END*, «$R, x_1, \ldots, x_n$, $+$», $+$» $\Leftrightarrow$
          $s \models$ «*CONTINUE*, «$R, x_1, \ldots, x_n$, $-$», $+$»]

Starting reading requires that all the reading you did before was part of other, past reading events, not part of the reading you now start. Ending your reading or finishing reading this book requires that any further reading you may do is not part of this reading event, but part of another, later reading event. These conditions on starting and ending/finishing capture just what it means for them to be transitions that flip the polarity in that type. They are encoded as conditional relations between supported types in (2.26). Despite the semantic similarities between resuming and starting, on the one hand, and between stopping and ending or finishing, on the other hand, the relations in (2.26) do not carry over to the aspectual verbs *resume* and *stop*.[11]

(2.26)   a. $\forall s, s'\ [s \models$ «*START*, T, $+$» and $s' \models T$, and s is part of
          $s' \Rightarrow \neg \exists s''\ [s'' \models PROG(T)$ and s'' is part of s' and s''
          precedes s]]

   b. $\forall s, s'\ [s \models$ «*FINISH*, T, $+$» and $s' \models T$, and s is part of
          $s' \Rightarrow \neg \exists s''\ [s'' \models PROG(T)$ and s'' is part of s' and s
          precedes s'']]

c. $\forall s, s'$ [$s \models$ «**END**, T, **+**» and $s' \models T$, and s is part of
$s' \Rightarrow \neg \exists s''$ [$s'' \models PROG(T)$ and s'' is part of s' and s
precedes s'']]

When Jane was reading, she must have started to read. After describing her reading with a past progressive, we need a perfect clause to describe the preceding onset of her reading. With a simple past tense description of her reading, *Jane read a book*, whose aspectual class is a filter, no shift to the perfect is necessary. We can continue with a simple past describing the plug that represents its onset (e.g., *She started at five o'clock*). Progressive descriptions presuppose that the start of the event preceded its current ongoing stage. A simple past tense carries no such presupposition, but we can infer that there must be a start and a finish to Jane's reading, represented as parts of Jane's reading only when we have any need to do so.

The start of an event and its end or finish distinguish the event in the continuous flow of time, separating it as an internally organized unit of change from whatever else is going on. Flipping the polarity in the embedded type effected by these aspectual verbs is just what is needed to characterize the aspectual classes. The holes are events that end, rather than finish, the filters finish, and the plugs require their start and finish to coincide, "locking up" their internal structure.

The aspectual verbs are themselves also related by negation, as long as their presuppositions are preserved. As long as you keep reading, you don't stop reading; and at the point where you don't keep reading, you stop reading. When you end your reading, you don't resume this reading again, after you have stopped it. When resume reading, you don't end your reading, even though you must have stopped it. When you finish reading something, you don't continue reading it; but as long as you continue reading it, you don't finish.

What about the external negation of *start*? English shows a lexical gap here, unless we accept intentional verbs like *refuse, reject*, or *refrain from* as lexicalizing the nonstart relation. Such intentional verbs are not assumed to belong to the class of aspectual verbs that describe the internal temporal structure of events. But in contexts where the lack of action and change needs to be described and explained, we often resort to the intentional stance, using static means to describe what is the case. Describing a situation in which something is not happening makes us attribute mental states to those who could have acted in it, but failed to do so. This external negation relates the pairs of aspectual verbs in (2.27).

(2.27)   stop/keep, finish/continue, resume/end, start/not-start

This external negation flips the polarity of the aspectual verb type itself, preserving the embedded type, representing the complement. These relations are represented as relations between types, now supported in the same situations, as shown in (2.28).

(2.28) a. $\forall s \, [s \models \text{«}STOP, T, +\text{»} \Leftrightarrow s \models \text{«}KEEP, T, -\text{»}]$
        b. $\forall s \, [s \models \text{«}FINISH, T, +\text{»} \Leftrightarrow s \models \text{«}CONTINUE, T, -\text{»}]$
        c. $\forall s \, [s \models \text{«}RESUME, T, +\text{»} \Leftrightarrow s \models \text{«}END, T, -\text{»}]$
        d. $\forall s \, [s \models \text{«}START, T, +\text{»} \Leftrightarrow$
            $s \models \text{«}NOT\text{-}START, T, -\text{»}]$

When the aspectual verbs are classified according to their own aspectual class, we have seen that the verbs describing beginning, resuming, stopping, and finishing are plugs, but *continue* and *keep* are holes. If we presuppose that an event has stopped, describing it as ending represents a hole, merely continuing its already negative phase. Combining internal complement negation with external negation on the aspectual verb itself, we see that *start* and *continue* are duals; that is, as long as you do not start not-reading, you must continue to read, all the time preserving the presupposition that you have started this reading. The analogy between existential and universal quantifiers in predicate logic is hence complete: just as $\exists$ and $\forall$ are duals, so the existential aspectual verbs and the quantificational ones are duals. There remains a difference in that ordinarily logical quantifiers carry no existential presuppositions, whereas all aspectual verbs do, except for *start* itself. This fundamental duality is extremely useful in explaining linguistic data.

Plugs have no distinguishable internal temporal structure, so they are insensitive to both kinds of polarity flips. They are self-dual, like proper names or individual constants in predicate logic. Since *start* is a plug, it can be used to illustrate this self-duality, allowing, only for the purposes of illustration, the momentary set-theoretic reduction of events to sets of plugs. A reading event may be reduced to a set R of stages of reading, including its start and its finish and all the situations s supporting the reading-type in between.

$$R = \{s \, | \, s \models \text{«}Read, x_1, +\text{»}\}$$

Taking out its starting stage, we get the set-theoretic complement of *start reading*, call it R^*.

$$R^* = \{s \, | \, s \models \text{«}Read, x_1, +\text{»}\} -$$
$$\{s \, | \, s \models \text{«}START, \text{«}Read, x_1, +\text{»}, +\text{»}\}$$

Taking the complement of R^* within R, we get back exactly the stage that supports its starting, a singleton set R^s.

$$R^s = R - R^* = \{s \, | \, s \models \text{«}START, \text{«}Read, x_1, +\text{»}, +\text{»}\}$$

In other words, the complement of the set of stages that do not constitute its start is exactly its starting point. It is important, of course, that in taking the complement we consider only the "local" stages of reading, already in R. All other places where reading is going on belong to other events and are contained in other contexts.

2.3 Monotonicity Properties

The aspectual verbs exhibit characteristic inferential patterns in simple inferences about events and their internal stages. If, for instance, you have started to read section 2.3 of this book, then you must have started to read this book. But if you have finished reading section 2.2, you need not have finished reading this book. By contrast, when you have finished the book, then you must also have finished its section 2.2. The existential aspectual verbs describing the onset of events allow inferences from parts to larger parts of the same event, increasing in the partial inclusion order; the verbs describing the ending of an event allow inferences from larger parts to smaller parts of the same event, decreasing in that partial order. This is a semantic correlate of the fact that these classes of aspectual verbs are interpreted by contrary relations, describing actions of turning an event-type on and turning it off. The terminology of generalized quantifier theory is espoused here for such inferential patterns with aspectual verbs.[12] When the inferences are valid from parts to larger parts, such verbs are *monotone increasing* in the type describing the event, representing the syntactic complement of the aspectual verb. When the inferences are valid from larger parts to smaller ones, such verbs are *monotone decreasing* in the type describing the event. The aspectual verbs *keep* and *continue* are accordingly also seen to be monotone increasing: if you continue or keep reading this section, you continue or keep reading this book, whereas the opposite obviously does not hold. These properties must be expressed in English using perfects, except for the already stative quantificational aspectual verbs. These tests of inferential patterns result in the following classification of monotonicity properties for aspectual verbs, where *T is part of T'* is the natural part-of relation between types:

(2.29)   a.   *Monotone increasing*
         Def. R_A represents a monotone-increasing aspectual verb iff

         $\forall s \ [s \models PERF\langle\langle R_A, T, +\rangle\rangle$, and T is part of $T' \Rightarrow$
         $s \models PERF\langle\langle R_A, T', +\rangle\rangle]$

         or for $R_A = keep, continue,$

         $\forall s \ [s \models \langle\langle R_A, T, +\rangle\rangle$, and T is part of $T' \Rightarrow$
         $s \models \langle\langle R_A, T', +\rangle\rangle]$

Inference examples in English:
i.   If Jane has started to read this section of the
      book ⇒ She has started to read this book
ii.   If Jane kept reading this section of the book ⇒
      She kept reading this book
Monotone-increasing aspectual verbs:
start, begin, initiate, commence, resume, continue, keep

b.   *Monotone decreasing*
      Def. R_A represents a monotone-decreasing aspectual
      verb iff

$$\forall s\ [s \models \textit{PERF}\ll R_A,\ T,\ +\gg,\ \text{and}\ T'\ \text{is part of}\ T \Rightarrow$$
$$s \models \textit{PERF}\ll R_A,\ T',\ +\gg]$$

Inference examples in English:
i.   If Jane has not started to read this book ⇒
      She has not started to read this section of the
      book
ii.   If Jane has stopped reading this book ⇒
      She has stopped reading this section of the book
iii. If the police ended the party ⇒
      The police ended the swimming at the party
Monotone-decreasing aspectual verbs:
finish, end, terminate, complete, cease, stop, not-start

Note again that in (2.29a(i), b(i), and b(ii)) the aspectual verbs that describe plugs require their stative perfect tense in the inferences. To see that a simple past inference with these verbs would not be valid, consider (2.30).

(2.30)   Jane started to read section 2.3 of this book ⇏
         Jane started to read this book

In (2.30) the simple past *Jane started to read section 2.3 of this book* describes the plug that is part of Jane's reading and that is, at least in natural situations, preceded by her starting to read this book. But one need not start reading a book by starting to read its first page. Starting to read a book in the middle does not violate any semantic presuppositions, but perhaps it transgresses some cultural conventions on the way we ordinarily proceed in reading. Reasoning with given information must ordinarily preserve the temporal reference, so (2.30) is invalid as a situated inference. The perfect tense inferences in (2.29) are valid, since they are entirely based on stative information that is independent of the current temporal reference. For the quantificational aspectual verbs that describe holes (i.e., *continue* and *keep*), as well as for some uses of *end*, the simple past inferences are valid, since holes preserve the current temporal reference. As may now be expected, the explicitly negative *not-start* also describes a hole, for negative types are supported throughout the event and their simple past inferences are valid (2.29b(i)).

But among the ending verbs, these tests do not yet distinguish the plugs described by *finish, complete,* and *stop* from the way we may use *end, cease,* and *discontinue,* presupposing a current negative stage and describing its continuation. Although we then describe the ending of an event, the context remains open for additional information about simultaneous events. Ending an activity requires first stopping it and then not resuming it—that is, flipping its internal polarity to negative and keeping it off. Clear and intuitive judgments reflecting this logical difference are hard to detect in English. Still, (2.31) may make the issues more tangible.

(2.31)   a.   The longer you keep reading, the sooner you'll finish.
         b.   The longer you keep reading, the later you'll end.

Finishing something means reaching an end that was determined to a certain extent at its outset. Finishing adds the plug into the available information that individuates the entire event as a unit in the continuous flow of time. In (2.31a) what it takes for you to finish reading is already determined beforehand. Hence, it is reached sooner by not interrupting your reading. But in (2.31b) the end of your reading is not determined until you stop your reading and do not resume it again. When that will be is presumably under your control. The more you read, the later you'll end, since as long as you keep reading, you have not ended. When you end what you are doing, you discontinue your action. Ending is a transition from having stopped to not resuming anymore (i.e., preserving a given state of non-action). Finishing or completing some event entails ending it, but not vice versa. In (2.32) the aspectual difference shows up in the nominalizations of these verbs. Endings are states within which other events take place, but finishings and completions are instantaneous plugs that cannot include other events.

(2.32)   a.   In the end it matters only what you say.
         b.   *In the finish/completion it matters only what you say.

Another manifestation of this difference in the aspectual verbs describing the last stages of events is illustrated in (2.33).

(2.33)   a.   I ended my lecture when the bomb exploded.
         b.   I finished my lecture when the bomb exploded.

In (2.33a) a causal property is attributed to the explosion: it put an end to my lecture or made me end my lecture. However, in (2.33b) the connection between the explosion and the end of the lecture is coincidental, since, presumably, finishing my lecture was an action I planned ahead of time, and the explosion was not.

Plugs control the flow of information by providing instantaneous transitions, closing the information gates, as it were, and forcing subsequent clauses to be interpreted as describing distinct later events. If aspectual verbs are represented explicitly as relations R_A between the given current event c and the embedded type T (i.e., R_A (c, T)), the plugs update c to a new c' preceded by c. Plugs are dynamic, affecting the contextually determined c in their left argument. The other aspectual verbs do not affect c, letting new information through the hole they represent. If plugs are dynamic context shifters, holes are static and preserve the current context.

One further linguistic effect of the monotonicity properties of aspectual verbs is observed in negative polarity contexts. It is well known that in NPs negative polarity is triggered by right-decreasing NPs, like *few N*, *none*, *hardly any N*, and *no N*. The right-decreasing aspectual verbs *stop*, *finish*, and *end* appear to trigger negative polarity *any*, too, as illustrated in (2.34).

(2.34) a. He ended any rumors about his past by telling the truth.
        b. Jane had stopped trying to make any sense out of the note.
        c. I have finished anything I had started.
        d. I did not start anything new.

The paraphrases of (2.34) in (2.35) make the incorporated negation in the right-decreasing aspectual verbs fully explicit.

(2.35) a. Rumors about his past no longer circulated after he had told the truth.
        b. Jane no longer tried to make sense of the note.
        c. I no longer have anything to do. I have nothing to do.
        d. I started nothing new.

This additional linguistic evidence attests to the right-decreasing properties of the aspectual verbs that describe turning off the ongoing action or its not starting, again requiring the dynamic ones to be expressed in perfect tense.

2.4 The Aspectual Cube

The monotonicity properties of the aspectual verbs and their relations to internal and external negation discussed in the preceding section are visualized in the aspectual cube in figure 2.1. It is important to understand this cube as visualizing a set of dynamic transitions, entering at *start* and exiting either at *end* or at *finish*. The double arrow patterns represent the dynamic plugs($\uparrow$)/stative holes($\downarrow$) distinction of the aspectual verbs and the

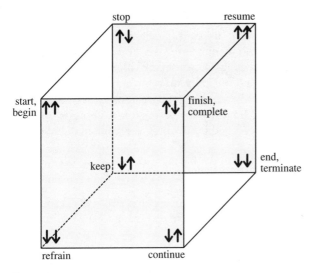

Figure 2.1
The aspectual cube

increasing(↑)/decreasing(↓) monotonicity in their complements. The top of the cube consists entirely of dynamic plugs that close the context, so that further episodic information must describe a later event (ignoring for the moment the possibility that the perspective may be refined; but see (2.37)). The bottom of the cube consists entirely of static holes that preserve the current context and let further information through as descriptive of simultaneous events. Although *end* and *terminate* may also be used as plugs, they are used as holes if it is presupposed that the action has already been turned off that is, if the interpretation has passed *stop*. Accordingly, four combinatory patterns of arrows are lexicalized in English, as shown in (2.36).

(2.36)   ↑↑: *start, resume, begin, initiate, commence*
         ↑↓: *stop, finish, complete*
         ↓↑: *keep, continue*
         ↓↓: *not-start, refrain from, end, cease, terminate, halt*

External negation flips the left arrow, making dynamic relations static and vice versa. All pairs listed in (2.27) are corners connected by a vertical top/bottom edge in the cube. Internal negation as polarity reversal in the complement preserves the dynamic or static nature of the aspectual relation, but flips the right arrow. All pairs listed in (2.17) are corners connected by horizontal edges of the cube.

For lexical self-dual plugs, like the descriptive verbs *knock, jump, arrive,* and the dynamic aspectual verbs themselves, the entire cube collapses into a point with no internal structure. This is logically on a par with the proper names in the NP category, which are equally self-dual and hence proper substitutions for variables bound by one of the pair of dual quantifiers. This accounts also for the fact that plugs are ordinarily blocked from complementing aspectual verbs (2.37a). But they may force an interpretation as hole with bare plural NPs (2.37b); a filter interpretation (2.37c); or a perspectival refinement, opening the plug for new internal information that presupposes that the action described by the plug is continuing (2.37d).

(2.37) a. *Jane started to arrive.
        b. People began to arrive.
        c. John finished jumping.
        d. Jane jumped over the fence. She started with a spurt, lifted her feet slowly from the ground, flew swiftly over the fence, . . .

The dynamic representation of the flow of information contains plugs that represent events as internally closed. But these may be represented as internally structured following perspectival refinement. This dynamic restructuring of plugs is analyzed in more detail in chapter 5, after the notion of perspective is given more specific content. In terms of the cube, a plug is represented as a self-dual point, collapsing all oppositions, but upon perspectival refinement it expands into a full-fledged cube with three-dimensional edges.

The aspectual cube provides a convenient way to visualize the internal composition of events and the semantic properties and relations of aspectual verbs describing it. When *start* is thought of as the unique point of entry into the cube, exiting in *end* makes the entire transition a hole; exiting in *finish*, however, makes it a filter. The back of the cube, the square consisting of *stop/resume/keep/end*, constitutes the fluid domain of measurable homogeneous quantity and plurality—the domain of holes, which are durative, continuous, and static objects that lack the internal structure to change the context and shift what the descriptive information is about. The front of the cube, the square consisting of *start/finish/not-start/continue*, makes up the individuated domain of individuals and of bounded events constituting a unit, despite the possibility of their being interrupted and having internal gaps.

The cube connects these two domains by transitions between its corners along the edges. The duality diagonals are free transitions, since they preserve the direction of the right arrow and affect only the dynamic/static status of the verb. For instance, if the point of entry into the cube is *start*, the transition to *keep* is free, merely preserving internal positive polarity. A horizontal transition switches the polarity to positive, if it is not already positive, or to negative, if it is not already negative. The rules for such

$+/-$ transitions are simply expressed in terms of the kinematics of arrows in (2.38), where the result of composing a transition is always identified by the last arrow. A $\downarrow$ represents a transition from on to off, whereas a $\uparrow$ represents a transition from off to on. For example, the first line in (2.38) is read as "composing a right-down arrow ($\downarrow$/off) with a right-up arrow ($\uparrow$/on) turns the event polarity to positive" (i.e., this line represents the start or resumption of the event).

(2.38)   *Arrow kinematics*
$$\downarrow + \uparrow = \uparrow$$
$$\uparrow + \downarrow = \downarrow$$
$$\downarrow + \downarrow = \downarrow$$
$$\uparrow + \uparrow = \uparrow$$

A more complex example is the transition described by the sequence *start/stop/resume/keep/stop/end* that amounts to the switching sequence *on/off/on/off*—a hole with one internal interruption, say, your studying temporal reasoning with one break to do something incompatible with it. A second example described by the sequence *start/keep/stop/continue/finish* is represented by the same switching sequence, *on/off/on/off*, but describes a filter with an interruption, say, your reading this book with a break to do something else. Note that *stop/continue* requires a transition through *resume*, for diagonally cutting across the center of the cube is not an admissible transition. This is due to the observed difference in the presuppositions of *keep* and *continue*, where *keep* preserves the given polarity of the embedded event-type, but *continue* switches it on, if it is not on (see section 2.1). Similarly, a transition from *start* directly to *end* is not admitted, but must pass through *stop* to introduce the plug turning it off. The presuppositions of *resume* are automatically projected since *start* is the only entry point, and all transitions between *start* and *resume* are accommodated in the context. So *on/off/on* is the switching sequence corresponding to *resume*, whereas for *start*, which has the same monotonicity properties and arrow pattern, the sequence is simply *on*. The vertical edges control the information flow, as gatekeepers changing or preserving the current temporal reference. The compositional kinematics of the left arrows also follows the rules in (2.38). As one would expect, the aspectual property of the verb last processed determines the control of the information flow. If you end where you have stopped, you create a hole. If you finish where you have stopped, you create a filter, blocking further information about the internal structure. Other transitions should now be evident.

Chapter 3
Dynamic Aspect Trees

Information about events is represented in directed graphs, called *dynamic aspect trees* (DATs), by nodes labeled with types encoding the descriptive information. These nodes are either open or closed, representing holes and plugs, respectively (i.e., letting further information through or blocking it). The rules for representing the information expressed by using English sentences are formulated in terms of constructive operations on given DATs that represent the current context. Reasoning with DATs models situated inferences about what happened, characterized by operations on DATs representing the information obtained from processing the premises. Section 3.4 contains a precise characterization of the syntactic and logical properties of DATs and their intended interpretation by embeddings into event structures that constitute structured representations of what was described as having happened.

3.1 Aspect as Control Structure

In chapter 1 we distinguished, besides the states that have no internal temporal structure, three aspectual classes of events: holes, filters, and plugs. These classes channel the flow of information about what happened. Holes let new information through, preserving the given temporal reference. Plugs block the flow and direct that further information must describe a later event. Filters are presently analyzed as giving an interpretive choice between holes and plugs, but chapter 5 will modify this interpretation importantly.

The aspectual class of complex linguistic expressions is determined compositionally. The mechanics of this process are deferred to chapter 6, where a fragment of English is given. As a rule of thumb, however, a description of an event is classified as a hole if at least one argument of the verb is indefinite, referring to a divisible object, or the intransitive verb itself describes a homogeneous action. Descriptions of events that have no such argument are classified as plugs or filters. The remaining clauses are classified as descriptions of states, using lexically stative verbs (e.g., *sit, own*), the copula *be*, or progressive or perfect verbal inflections. The syntax of the fragment in chapter 6 determines the argument structure of the lexical verbs and codes their divisibility in terms of arrows. Composition of the aspectual classes is computed according to the arrow kinematics rules from section 2.4. The present section introduces the basic ideas of DATs as representational tools for temporal anaphora, assuming that each type, coding the descriptive information contained in a linguistic clause, comes classified for its aspectual class. Holes will correspond to open nodes; plugs will correspond to closed nodes.

An event of issuing information, orally or otherwise, terminates the past. We will call this event the *source*, which provides the first parameter of context-dependence in temporal reasoning and determines its perspective, as discussed in more detail in chapter 5. A DAT must contain a unique node representing this source, labeled by the type «*SOURCE*, x, $+$». It is always constructed as the rightmost terminal node in a DAT, a plug, for we disregard here whatever internal structure the act of issuing information may have. Any information expressed using a past tense is to be interpreted as describing events preceding this source node and is represented in a DAT as nodes on a branch to the left of the source. Present tense reports are, of course, to be interpreted as describing events that temporally include this source. The use of the auxiliary verbs *will* or *would* in narrative texts is regarded as a form of modality requiring information about admissible alternatives as modal base. The tools of DAT representation are especially designed for temporal reasoning about the described past as intended application, excluding modalities and counterfactuals.

The nodes in a DAT are connected by downward arrows intended to represent the temporal inclusion relation between events. An arrow from a higher labeled node to a lower labeled node means that the event supporting the type labeling the lower node happened within the time of the event supporting the type labeling the higher node. This relation between events is merely temporal inclusion, not spatial inclusion, though it may, depending on the part-whole relation between its constituents, also happen to imply spatial inclusion.

The left-to-right order between such paths of connected nodes within a DAT reflects the flow of time. If node n_1 on a path is to the left of another node n_2 on a distinct path, then n_1 represents an event that occurred before the event represented by n_2. This temporal precedence order is a strict partial order.

Every DAT is rooted in one single root node, dominating all other nodes including the source node. This root node represents the entire episode described by the linguistic material processed. It is a hole, for obvious reasons, although we could convert it to a plug upon terminating the information flow. If DATs are sometimes displayed without these source and root nodes, for simplicity, they should nevertheless be thought of as implicitly present.

Every DAT has a node that was the last one constructed in the process of interpretation, its *current node*. This node represents in the DAT what was previously informally called the temporal reference point or the current event. The open/closed nature of this current node determines how the given DAT must be updated with further information. If it is an open node, representing a hole, the DAT grows an arrow descending from it to a new dependent node. If it is closed, representing a plug, the DAT grows a new node descending from one of its parent nodes, dominating the current one. There may be a choice of dominating nodes from which to grow a new one. This apparent indeterminacy in the interpretation is constrained by the compatibility conditions of types. Ordinarily, the lowest dominating node compatible with the new information must be the parent node dominating the new node. Below we discuss in more detail what enters into this process of determining where the new node should be located and how it affects the inferential relations and perspectival information.

Simple past tense clauses describing events introduce new nodes, and only such clauses make the DAT in which they are interpreted grow. Quantificational relations or simple past tense clauses containing information about states, often using the auxiliary *be* or *have* or lexical stative verbs, do not introduce new nodes. A type classified as a state is introduced in a DAT as a *sticker*, appended either to the label of the current node, if it is a plug, or to the next node, if the current one is a hole. Perfect clauses, using the auxiliary verb *have* with a past participle main verb, describe perfect states and do not introduce new nodes in a DAT either. Their content is represented as a sticker by the type $PERF\langle\!\langle R, x, +\rangle\!\rangle$, representing the state of x having R-ed. Progressive clauses also do not introduce new nodes; instead, they append the type $PROG\langle\!\langle R, x, +\rangle\!\rangle$, representing the state of R-ing, as a sticker. All forms of stative information are treated on the same principle: they do not make the DAT grow, but append a possibly conditional type according to the sticker rule (see chapter 4). Unlike the ordinary types labeling nodes that represent events, such stickers are portable; that is, they can be transmitted to other nodes when the DAT grows. This captures the fact that the information they contain may serve as background when a new node is grown that is independent of the current one. The different conditions on the portability of stative information encoded in stickers are described in chapter 4, capturing their different roles in reasoning. Stative information hence has two semantic characteristics: first, it does not introduce new nodes in a DAT, and second, it is portable and projected from the node that it initially labels.

3.2 DATs for Texts

DATs represent the descriptive, aspectual, and perspectival information that results from the interpretation of English discourse or texts. Let us assume that the linguistic input is parsed into basic constituent structure, where the lexical expressions in the structured strings are assigned syntactic categories. The syntactic rules for the simple fragment of English considered here are given in chapter 6.

The verbal head of an inflected phrase, categorially IP, is represented as the main descriptive relation with its argument structure. Descriptive material in other categories is represented in types restricting the parameters in the arguments. The rationale for this structure of types representing clauses is that the verbal head requires that the situation it describes contain the relation described by V. NPs, PPs, and adjuncts may, but need not, describe constituents of this situation. They may describe constituents of other situations contributed via the parameter to the situation described by the verbal head. Restrictions on parameters need not be part of what is described in the situation described by the verbal head, though the parameters themselves are. The category Infl contains the constraints on the temporal referential relations of the types, aspectual information, and the polarity assignment. Further discussion and a systematic account of the mapping of syntactic form into types is deferred to the fragment in chapter 6.

The first example of how a DAT is constructed by the process of interpretation is based on the sequence of sentences originally displayed in (1.1).

(1.1)   A car hit the fence. The driver was killed. The police arrived.

We begin the interpretation of (1.1) by designing a DAT representing the source node as a plug dominated by the root, a hole. The source, from which the information was issued, is constrained to remain the rightmost node in every extension of this DAT. The first sentence, *A car hit the fence*, is interpreted as expressing the descriptive information coded in the type

$$\langle\!\langle HIT, x_{\langle\!\langle CAR, x, +\rangle\!\rangle}\, y_{\langle\!\langle FENCE, y, +\rangle\!\rangle}\, +\rangle\!\rangle$$

Both indefinite and definite NPs are represented as restrictions on parameters that are arguments of the **HIT** relation. The definiteness of *the fence* requires that the parameter y be identified with an old parameter already used before this point of the interpretation, or possibly identified with an appropriate object in the source situation. For simplicity, this definiteness requirement is not made explicit here, but it is straightforward to incorporate it as a constraint (see the rule for definite determiners in chapter 6).[1] The simple past tense requires that the described event precede the issuing of the information. In the DAT a branch (or path) is constructed to the left

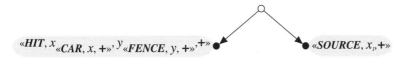

Figure 3.1
First partial DAT for (1.1)

of the source, with a new node labeled by the type representing the descriptive information. The new node itself is closed, representing a plug. The DAT now contains three nodes: the source, the root, and the current node, the last one constructed. Further information cannot be encoded as a type labeling a node dependent on the current one, but should label a new right-sister node dependent on the root. The DAT resulting from the interpretation of the first sentence of (1.1) is displayed in figure 3.1.

The descriptive information expressed in the second sentence in (1.1), *The driver was killed*, is represented by the type

$$\text{«KILL, } z, v_{\text{«DRIVE}, v, x, \text{+»}}, \text{ +»}$$

The passive clause is first converted to its active form and represented as a relation between two new parameters z and v, v restricted to refer to the driver of the car, using x introduced in the interpretation of the first sentence. Again the definiteness of *the driver* should be made explicit by an identity condition in its type that constrains its reference to corefer with a suitable given parameter. The parameter x is picked up as the second parameter of the relation *drive*, to constrain the driver to be the driver of the car that hit the fence. The type labels a new node in the DAT that now becomes the current node, another plug, that is a right sister to the former current one. The resulting DAT is given in figure 3.2. Note that the past tense of the second sentence does not have any temporal referential force in the interpretation of the second sentence. Its semantic role is merely to constrain its reference to an event that precedes the source. The context represented in the DAT and its current node determine how the event referred to by the second sentence is located in time with respect to the events already represented in the DAT. Some natural languages do not mark tense on clauses, except for the first one, in such a temporal anaphoric chain of events.[2] In this dynamic view of interpretation, that seems a very efficient communicative strategy for expressing temporal reference in a language.

The last sentence in (1.1), *The police arrived*, is now interpreted. It is represented by a third closed node, sister to the current one and to the left of the source. Its label is

$$\text{«ARRIVE, } w_{\text{«POLICE}, w, \text{+»}}, \text{ +»}$$

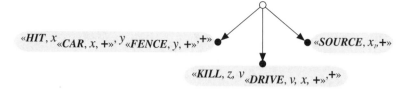

Figure 3.2
Second partial DAT for (1.1)

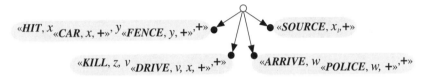

Figure 3.3
Complete DAT for (1.1)

The resulting DAT represents this event as a plug as well. The node is located as a right sister to the given current one and as a left sister to the source node, satisfying the simple-past tense constraint. Figure 3.3 contains the final DAT for (1.1).

When we compare this DAT for (1.1) with the DAT that represents the closely related (1.11),

(1.11)   The car hit the fence. The driver had been killed. The police arrived.

the important difference in the dynamics of simple past tense versus stative perfect tense is clarified. The only difference between (1.1) and (1.11) is that the second clause in the latter uses a past perfect tense (*The driver had been killed*) instead of a simple past. Perfect tenses are represented by the type *PERF«T, +»* that is appended as sticker to the label of either the current node, if it is a plug, or the next node introduced, if the current node is a hole. Perfect tense clauses are descriptions of perfect states and hence do not introduce new nodes that make the DAT grow. The DAT resulting from interpreting (1.11) is given in figure 3.4.

The DAT in figure 3.4 contains a conjoined label on the leftmost node, which represents the information that at the time the car hit the fence the driver had already been killed. Despite their static nature, the textual order in which perfect tense clauses are given still matters; for the DAT in figure 3.5, representing (1.13),

(1.13)   The car hit the fence. The police arrived. The driver had been killed.

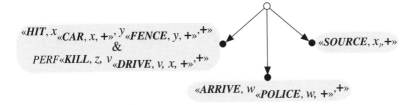

Figure 3.4
DAT for (1.11)

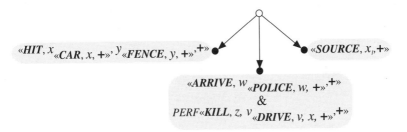

Figure 3.5
DAT for (1.13)

where the perfect clause *The driver had been killed* comes last, differs from figure 3.4 in the node that carries the perfect sticker.

From (1.11), but not from (1.13), we infer (1.12).

(1.12) The driver was killed before his car hit the fence and before the police arrived.

If what happened is correctly described by (1.13) instead, the killing of the driver could well have taken place after the car hit the fence, but before the police arrived. That course of events is not a possible interpretation for (1.11), since the perfect tense requires that the event that caused the perfect state have ended before the given temporal reference. For (1.11) to be true, the killing of the driver must have ended before the car hit the fence, leaving open the question of what killed him. In section 3.3 we will return to the use of perfect tense conclusions in reasoning with DATs.

As discussed in chapter 1, (1.2) describes three simultaneous actions performed by Jane, while being happy.

(1.2) Jane was so happy. She sang, danced, and clapped her hands.

The DAT construction for (1.2) proceeds as follows. First the basic source and root nodes are constructed, exactly as for (1.1). Next the state described by *Jane was so happy* must be represented. As the DAT contains no

Figure. 3.6
First partial DAT for (1.2)

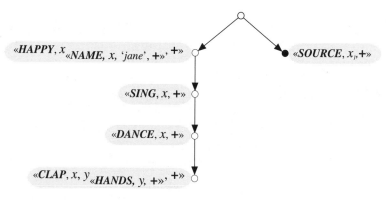

Figure. 3.7
DAT for (1.2)

node to the left of the source, a new node must be introduced in this case, because the simple past tense requires a node to the left of the source node. In this special case the stative information is not simply appended as a sticker; the constraint of the simple past tense here has a dynamic effect in the DAT, growing a new node.[3] This node is a hole labeled by the type

$$\text{«}HAPPY, x_{\text{«}NAME, x, 'jane', +\text{»}}, +\text{»}$$

where the proper name *Jane* is represented by the restricted parameter x, which is required to refer to an object so named, presumably in an earlier situation.[4] Note that the copula carrying the inflection and aspectual information is not represented by a descriptive relation in the type. It contributes to the control information in requiring a hole to the left of the source. The DAT at this point looks like figure 3.6. The second sentence contains three main verbs in coordination, all describing holes. They are represented on one continuing path dependent upon the left node in figure 3.6. The full DAT for (1.2) is given in figure 3.7.

Had the DAT been constructed for (1.3), which differs from (1.2) only in that the second clause is modified by *consecutively*, it would have had three holes represented as sisters dependent on the current node in the first partial DAT for (1.2). In this case adverbial quantificational structure con-

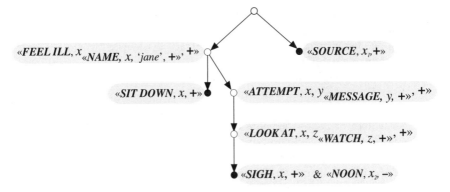

Figure 3.8
First DAT for (1.5)

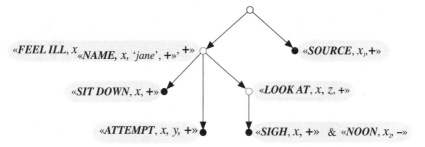

Figure 3.9
Second DAT for (1.5)

structs a context to represent the holes as sister nodes, overruling their aspectual information, just like the causal constraint can do.

The next example of a text to illustrate DAT construction is (1.5).

(1.5)   Jane felt ill. She sat down, attempted to decipher the message, and looked at her watch. She sighed. It was not even noon yet.

Two DATs are generated by interpreting (1.5), one where Jane's attempt to decipher the message, a filter, is represented as a hole (figure 3.8) and one where it is interpreted as a plug (figure 3.9). Both DATs are given as completed representations with somewhat abbreviated types. From figure 3.8 we infer, for instance, that Jane sighed after sitting down, while feeling ill and attempting to decipher the message. *Looking at* something—say, one's watch or the sunset—is always interpreted as a hole, as opposed to the static perception verb *see*. Only if the next clause contains incompatible information can the introduction of a new sister node be forced. But if we instead interpret (1.5) with a causal constraint to understand that Jane stopped her attempt to decipher the message in order to look at her watch —perhaps a natural interpretation—that attempt must be represented as a plug, and, consequently, Jane's sigh must have occurred after her attempt, as in figure 3.9. Note that in both figure 3.8 and figure 3.9 the stative information that it was not yet noon is represented as a sticker, appending the negative type to the plug introduced by the previous clause. In chapter 4 we will further refine the rules for stickers and will discuss the "portability" of such labels, transmitting them to other nodes than the one they were originally appended to when the stative information was obtained.

Suppose now that we continue (1.5) with (1.15a).

(1.15) a. Jane left the station. She was now ready to call. She saw a phone booth, and was taking money out of her wallet. Then she found the note again.

Given that the current node in both figure 3.8 and figure 3.9 is a plug, the interpretation proceeds by first backing up to the hole representing Jane's looking at her watch. The question that arises is whether Jane is still looking at her watch, while leaving the station.[5] For commonsense reasons, it may be unlikely that she keeps looking at her watch, while leaving the station. If a semantic theory is connected to a module representing commonsense knowledge, the interpretation can exploit such rules in DAT construction. But in this context we also know that Jane looked at her watch after she sat down, that is, while seated. Now the new information entails that she is moving; hence, she is no longer seated. Consequently, her leaving the station is not a temporal part of her looking at her watch, or of her attempt to decipher the message, but it should be preceded by both. Maintaining compatibility of the information encoded in the labels or their entailments, the node for Jane's leaving the station should depend only on the higher hole representing her feeling ill. In both cases we infer that Jane is still feeling ill, as she is leaving the station. The two resulting DATs are given in figures 3.10 and 3.11.

Introducing a new node independent of the current one is part of a shift of perspective. The new perspective is constructed by the plug rule and by the general principle that the types on one branch and their entailments must be compatible. The lowest node compatible with the new information serves as parent to the new node, ensuring also that the new information is compatible with any higher ancestor node on the path to the root of the DAT. Such paths connecting a set of labeled nodes to the root in a DAT are called *chronoscopes*. They will turn out to be very useful instruments in temporal reasoning with DATs, as we will see in section 3.4. Chronoscopes are essential tools for situated reasoning, representing both the local con-

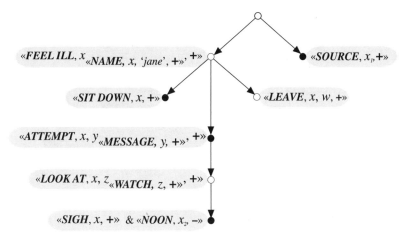

Figure 3.10
First DAT for (1.5) + first sentence of (1.15a)

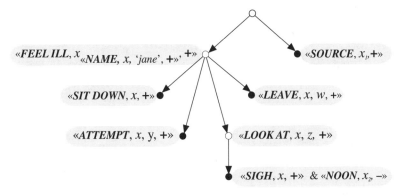

Figure 3.11
Second DAT for (1.5) + first sentence of (1.15a)

text for updating and the information from stickers imported into them from other chronoscopes in the DAT. A chronoscope is called the *current chronoscope* just in case it contains the current node.

Compatibility of information is determined partly lexically, and partly by the entailment relations between types within the same chronoscope. Obviously a type with a positive polarity is incompatible with a type that is constituted of the same relation and parameters but contains a negative polarity. As a relation between types, compatibility is obviously reflexive, symmetric, and transitive. Furthermore, if T is compatible with T' and with T'' independently, and T' is compatible with T'', then T must be compatible with T' & T''.

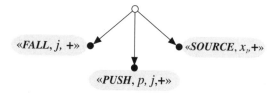

Figure 3.12
DAT for a text with two simple past tense plugs

Figure 3.13
DAT for causal interpretation

Figure 3.14
DAT for simple past tense plug and perfect sticker

Backing up in a chronoscope to create a new one in a perspectival shift is a recursive process. It terminates at the lowest ancestor node of the given current node labeled with compatible information, while plugging its child (i.e., the child of the lowest ancestor node) carrying information that was incompatible. The creation of a new chronoscope in shifting the perspective requires a certain amount of reasoning, checking the compatibility of information and various inferential processes. At this point the interpreter may use reasoning rules that are not semantic in nature, but based on causal regularities or other constraints. The DATs for a text with two simple past tenses, *John fell. Peter pushed him*, where the second can be interpreted as describing the event that causes the one described first, are given in figures 3.12 through 3.14. The issues that arise in the course of such reasoning while shifting the perspective are dealt with in more detail in section 3.4 and in chapter 5 on perspectives.

Based on these examples of how the interpretation of a text constructs DATs, the following rules may now be formulated:

(3.1)   *Rules for DAT representation of aspectual classes*
1.   Sticker rule
      If the new information is a state-type, append the type
      as a sticker to the current node, if it is a plug, and
      append it to the next node, if the current node is a hole.
2.   Hole rule
      If the new information is an activity-type, introduce a
      new hole, make it the current node, and label it with
      the new type.
3.   Filter rule
      If the new information is an accomplishment-type,
      introduce either a hole or a plug, make it the current
      node, and label it with the new type.
4.   Plug rule
      If the new information is an achievement-type, introduce
      a plug, make it the current node, and label it with the
      new type.
5.   Filler rule
      If the extension of the DAT resulting from applying
      rules 1–4 is inconsistent,[6] then plug the closest
      dominating node necessary to remove the inconsistency,
      make it the current node, and reapply the rules.

As we have seen, the nature of the current node determines where the new
node is located. For future reference, these rules are stated in (3.2).

(3.2)   *Update rules for DATs*
1.   Hole update
      If the current node is a hole, represent the new node as
      its child.
2.   Plug update
      If the current node is a plug, represent the new node as
      its sister.

The discussion in chapter 2 of the relation between aspectual verbs and
the aspectual classes led us to conclude that holes are internally structured
as transitions from *start* via *stop* to *end;* that is, the left arrow of the composed transition is down. In terms of DAT representation, such transitions
require the given current chronoscope to be preserved either by appending
any new information as a sticker or by introducing a child of its current
node. Filters give the choice of either representing the new information as
a hole, allowing further descent into the given chronoscope, or terminating
the given chronoscope. In the latter case new information is represented in
a new chronoscope, by backing up and plugging the node whose parent is

the lowest node representing the information shared with the new chronoscope. Creating a perspectival shift reverses the direction of the left arrow on this node, as it is being plugged, from ↓ to ↑. Plugging of an internally structured node hides its internal structure, rendering it inaccessible in the shifted perspective to the new current chronoscope. The observable linguistic manifestation of this plugging is that all the information labeling the inaccessible nodes must now be reported by means of perfect tense, unless it is represented in stickers that may be transmitted to a node in the new current chronoscope. Plugs, terminating a chronoscope, are self-dual in terms of the aspectual cube of section 2.4. They have no internal structure in the given perspective, though, as discussed in chapter 5, a perspectival refinement is always possible, opening the plug to render its internal structure accessible.

3.3 Reasoning with DATs: Chronoscopes

Constructing DATs models the accumulation of information in processing natural-language input. In reasoning with DATs, we rely on a fundamental property of the situations that support them, called *persistence*. If a situation s_1 supports DAT_1, for instance, and DAT_2 grows out of DAT_1 by application of the rules formulated above, and s_2 supports DAT_2, then s_2 supports DAT_1. Persistence means that the information represented at an earlier stage of construction of a DAT is never lost when the interpretation is continued, although the nodes may not remain accessible from any later current node. The way the available information may be reported in natural-language conclusions depends on the current node in the DAT and its relation to the node labeled with the descriptive information the conclusion is using. The given DAT may be affected by incorporating new information, not merely by growing new nodes, but also by plugging holes or opening plugs for perspectival refinement. The interpretation defines a nonmonotonic update relation between DATs, because a DAT need not be preserved as a substructure of what it grows into.

In chapter 1 the list of inferences based on (1.1) was given in (1.9) (* indicates invalid inference).

(1.1)   The car hit the fence. The driver was killed. The police arrived.

(1.9)   a.   The car hit the fence before the driver was killed.
        b.   *The car hit the fence when/after the driver was killed.
        c.   The driver was killed when/after the car had hit the fence.
        d.   The car had hit the fence before/when the driver was killed.

e. *The driver had been killed after/while the car hit the fence.
f. The police arrived after the driver was killed.
g. The police arrived when the driver was dead.
h. The police arrived when the car had hit the fence.
i. The car having hit the fence, the police arrived.

The completed DAT for (1.1) was given in figure 3.3, repeated here. Its current node is the one carrying the information that the police arrived, that is, the immediate left sister of the source. The conclusions of a situated inference also describe the current node, if the argument is valid. In this sense, reasoning with the information represented in a DAT always depends upon the current node, making the temporal reasoning paradigmatic of situated reasoning. The current node is the point of departure, as it were, in the process of attempting to verify the conclusion. For (1.9a) to be true, given the DAT in figure 3.3 for (1.1), there must be a node in the current chronoscope dominating the two nodes labeled with the information expressed by simple past tense clauses. The adverbial *before* constrains the relation between these nodes with this common ancestor: the node representing the car hitting the fence should be a left descendant of the ancestor that it has in common with the node representing the driver getting killed.[7] This is obviously the case in figure 3.3: the common ancestor is the root, and the node representing the car hitting the fence is indeed its left descendant relative to the node representing the killing of the driver. If instead the clause-linking adverbial had been *when* or *after*, as in (1.9b), the conclusion would not follow from the DAT in figure 3.3, since *when* or *after* would require the hitting node to be in the same chronoscope as the killing node or to be a right descendant of its common ancestor, respectively.

In (1.9c–e) the perfect clause describes the enduring perfect state that began after the hitting. That state is represented by appending a sticker to the current node when we interpret the conclusion. The adverb *when* requires that the related nodes be in the same chronoscope. When *after* is the temporal connector with the perfect clause, the state is required to have started before the event reported in the simple past tense clause started.

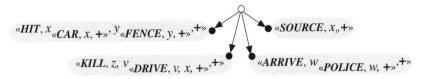

Figure 3.3
Complete DAT for (1.1)

Using *before/when* with simple past tense, as in (1.9d), is similar, when the main clause is in perfect tense. But, as is evident in (1.9e), a sticker describing the perfect state with a positive polarity resulting from an event cannot be imported into an earlier (left) chronoscope.[8]

In verifying a perfect tense conclusion, the interpreter searches for the lowest node in the intersection of the current chronoscope with a chronoscope containing a left-descendant node labeled with the corresponding type. The DAT representation facilitates a rather simple, systematic, and always-terminating search algorithm.

> 1. Back up to the first node dominating the current node and see whether it is contained in any chronoscope containing the desired node.
> 2. If so, the conclusion is verified.
> 3. If not, back up to the next higher node in the current chronoscope.
> 4. Repeat until the entire DAT is searched.
> 5. If the conclusion has not been verified, the argument is invalid.

In verifying (1.9f–i), the interpreter labels the current node with the information that the police arrived. All that needs verifying is that this node is a right descendant of a common ancestor of the node representing the killing (1.9f). The causal consequences of that node (i.e., the state of the driver's being dead) are stickers imported into the current chronoscope (1.9g), and the current chronoscope intersects with the one containing the node that the car hit the fence (1.9h). For the progressive perfect conclusion in (1.9i) we need to verify that the nonprogressive perfect type labels a node in the current chronoscope. Simple progressive conclusions require that an ancestor of the current node (i.e., in the current chronoscope) be labeled with the descriptive type or with $PROG(T)$ again, possibly imported from an earlier chronoscope. Such conclusions are good examples of situated inferences because, as discussed in chapter 5, they are not ordinarily preserved in perspectival shifts.

In chapter 1 the inferences from (1.2) were listed in (1.10), (again, * indicates invalid inference).

> (1.2)   Jane was so happy. She sang, she danced, and she clapped her hands.

> (1.10)   a.   Jane danced while clapping her hands.
>   b.   Jane was happy when/while she danced.
>   c.   While Jane was dancing, she was happy.
>   d.   *While Jane was happy, she was dancing.

The DAT for (1.2) was presented in figure 3.7, repeated here; its current node is the lowest hole, representing Jane's clapping. At this node the

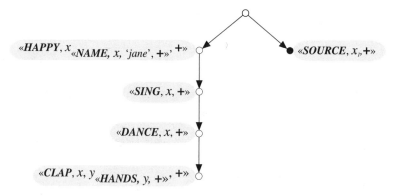

Figure 3.7
DAT for (1.2)

conclusions are represented as types in its label and verified. On the basis of this DAT, the inferences in (1.10) can be verified as follows. The adverb *while* in (1.10a) connects a progressive clause to a simple past main clause. It requires the clapping and the dancing to be at least partly simultaneous. In the DAT the node representing the clapping is the current node and it is a child of the node representing the dancing, so (1.10a) is verified. The adverbs *when* and *while* in (1.10b) describe the same temporal relation when connecting two simple past tenses. But (1.10c) and (1.10d) show that *while* S requires an event or state that is entirely included in the event or state described by the simple past main clause. Since the dancing is dominated by the node representing the state of Jane's being happy, (1.10c) is verified, but (1.10d) is not, for it would require Jane to keep dancing for as long as she is happy.

These examples illustrate how situated inferences use a DAT representation of the information given in the premises. Reasoning with a DAT consists of systematic operations or procedures to verify conclusions at its current node. This operationalization of inferential processes clarifies the advantage that such graphic representations of information have over mere symbolic logical-form representations. The form of a DAT and the location of its current node provide a systematic search procedure, guaranteed to terminate either in a verification or in a rejection of the conclusion. Conclusions never add new nodes to the given DAT for their premises, but their types are appended to the current node, if they prove to be valid. In the next section the intended semantic interpretation of DATs is presented in terms of embeddings into event structures, which satisfy additional domain-specific constraints for temporal reasoning. This leads to the proper characterization of situated entailment as a relation between premises and conclusion of an inference in terms of embeddings of the DAT that represents the information contained in the premises.

3.4 DATs: Their Syntax and Semantics

In order to consider DATs as structured objects in their own right, we should determine what forms they may take by specifying the syntactic conditions on their well-formedness. DATs are structured semantic objects constrained by certain formation principles; they are not expressions of any language that encode the "logical form" of the natural-language input into a language designed to represent its meaning.

Types that label the nodes of a DAT are formed by the following rules, recursively specifying the class of types *TYPE*:

(3.3)   *Definition of TYPE*
   i. T is a *basic* type in *TYPE* iff T is a sequence consisting of an *n*-ary relation R, n objects $a_1, \ldots, a_n$, and a positive or negative polarity $+$ or $-$.
   ii. T is a *parametric* or *parameterized* type in *TYPE* iff T is a basic type in which a relation or an object is replaced by a relation parameter R or an object parameter a_i, respectively.
   iii. If T is in *TYPE* and x is an object parameter, then x_T is a restricted object parameter. If T contains x_T, then T is a *restricted parametric type* in *TYPE*.
   iv.   If x is a parameter and T is in *TYPE*, then $[x|T]$ is a *role*. If T is a restricted parametric type, all parameters in the restriction must occur in the role to the left of $|$.[9]
   v.   If T and T' are in *TYPE*, then so are the *conjoined type* «T & T'» and the *conditional type* «$T \Rightarrow T'$».
   vi.   Nothing else is in *TYPE* unless it is obtained by the clauses in (i)–(v).

There is a fundamental notion, already encountered in section 3.3, of *compatibility* of types. Any two types are compatible iff there is a situation that supports both within the same chronoscope. Obviously, any type is compatible with itself and incompatible with its negative counterpart with a negative polarity or any of its entailments. Knowledge of the world supplies a host of basic (in)compatibility relations between types, which may be encoded as constraints in the lexicon.[10] Two sets of types are compatible iff their union is compatible; and a single type T is compatible with a set S of types just in case $S \cup \{T\}$ is compatible.

(3.4)   *Definition of DAT*
A DAT consists of

i.   a finite set of nodes, $N = \{n, n', \dots, n_m\}$,

ii.   a function δ_N from N to N^*, where N^* is the set of nonrepeating finite sequences of N, assigning to each node n a sequence of nodes, its children or immediate dependents $\delta_N(n)$,

iii. a function π_N from N to N, assigning an arrow pointing to a node n from its immediately dominating node, its parent $\pi_N(n)$,[11]

iv.   a subset H_N of N, the holes; $N - H_N$ is the set P_N of plugs,

v.   a function α_N from N to the powerset of $TYPE$, assigning to each node a set of types,[12]

vi.   a distinguished node c_N in N, the current node, and another distinguished node s_N in P_N, the source node,

such that

1. $\forall n, n'$ in N, n is in $\delta_N(n')$ iff $\pi_N(n) = n'$.

2.   There is one and only one node, the root, that is its own ancestor (n is an ancestor of n' iff $\exists n_1, \dots, n_m$ ($m \geq 2$) such that $n_i = \pi_N(n_{i+1})$, $n = n_1$ and $n' = n_m$).

3.   The source node is the terminal plug of the rightmost chronoscope.

4.   The set of all types labeling the ancestors of any node n (i.e., $\cup \{\alpha_N(n') | n'$ is an ancestor of $n\}$) is compatible with those types labeling n itself.

Information accumulation is simulated by updating a DAT. It is defined as an ordering on DATs as in (3.5).

(3.5)   *Updating a DAT*
DAT D_1 is updated to DAT D_2 iff $D_1 < D_2 = D_1 \cup \{c_{D_2}\}$ and either

1.   Hole rule
c_{D_1} is in H_{D_1} and each of $\delta_{D_2}, \pi_{D_2}, H_{D_2}$, and α_{D_2} extends the corresponding function of D_1 with the single exception that $\delta_{D_2}(c_{D_1}) = \langle c_{D_2} \rangle$, or

2.   Plug rule
c_{D_1} is in P_{D_1} and each of $\delta_{D_2}, \pi_{D_2}, H_{D_2}$, and α_{D_2} extends the corresponding function of D_1, with the single exception that $\delta_{D_2}(\pi_{D_1}(c_{D_1}))$ is obtained by appending c_{D_2} to the end of $\delta_{D_1}(\pi_{D_1}(c_{D_1}))$, or

3. Filler rule

   $\alpha_{D_2}(c_{D_2})$ is incompatible with the types assigned to the ancestors of c_{D_1}; and $\exists D_1' < D_2$ with the same nodes as D_1 and the same functions δ, π, and α but with $c_{D_1'}$ as ancestor of c_{D_1} and $c_{D_1'}$ is not in $H_{D_1'}$.

4. Sticker rule

   c_{D_1} is in N_{D_1} and each of δ_{D_2}, π_{D_2}, N_{D_2} is identical to its corresponding function of D_1, but α_{D2} extends the corresponding function of D_1 and $c_{D_1} = c_{D_2}$ if c_{D_1} is in P_{D_1}, and otherwise α_{D_2} is extended into α_{D_3} after application of the hole or filler rule.

Define $\ll$ to be the transitive closure of $<$; that is, $D \ll D'$ iff there are $D_1, \ldots, D_n$ such that $D_i < D_{i+1}$, $D = D_1$, and $D' = D_n$.

Let 0 be the DAT with a single node o, $\delta_0(o) = \langle o \rangle$, $\pi_0(o) = o$, $H_0(o) = o$, $c_0(o) = o$, $\alpha_0(o) = \varnothing$. The class of *well-formed* DATs consists of only those DATs D such that $0 \ll D$.

DATs are intended to be interpreted in event structures, consisting of events with their natural temporal inclusion and precedence ordering and constrained by some special temporal conditions. We first define the notion of an event frame.

(3.6) *Definition of event frame*

An *event frame* consists of a set of events E ordered by temporal inclusion $\rightarrow$ ($x \rightarrow y$ — y is a temporal part of x) and temporal precedence $<$ ($x < y$ — x occurs before y), together with an assignment to each T in *TYPE* of a set of events $[\![T]\!]$, the *extension* of T, such that the temporal inclusion is a partial order, temporal precedence is a strict partial order, and their interaction is constrained by[13]

• *monotonicity*: if $y \rightarrow x$ and $y < z$, then $x < z$

• *convexity*: if $x < y < z$ and $u \rightarrow x$ and $u \rightarrow z$, then $u \rightarrow y$

DATs are interpreted in such event frames by embeddings, mapping nodes to events preserving the temporal relations and satisfying certain additional conditions.

(3.7) *Definition of embedding*

A function f mapping a DAT into an event frame is an *embedding* iff

i.   for every arrow $\pi_N(n) \rightarrow n$, $f(\pi_N(n)) \rightarrow f(n)$,

ii. if n c-commands n', then $f(n) < f(n')$,[14]

iii. $f(n) \models T$, where T is the type labeling n.

The event frames into which DATs are embedded are called *event structures*. They are suitable models for temporal reasoning if they in addition satisfy at least the following constraints.

(3.8)   *Semantic constraints for temporal reasoning*
1.   Maximality of event-types
      If $e \models T$ and e is part of e' and $e' \models T$, then $e = e'$.
2.   Downward persistence for states/stickers
      If $e \models T$, T is a sticker, and e' is part of e, then $e' \models T$.
3.   If T is part of T', then $\forall e$ if $e \models PROG(T)$, then
      $e \models PROG(T')$.
4. $e \models PERF(T)$ iff $\exists e' < e$, $e' \models T$.
5.   If $e \models T$ and e' is part of e, then $e' \models PROG(T)$.
6.   If $e \models PROG(T)$ and T is classified as a hole, then $e \models T$.
7.   If $e < e'$, then $e < \text{start}(e')$.
8. $e \models START(T)$ iff $\exists e'$ $[e' \models T$ and $e = \text{start}(e')]$.
9. $\forall e$ if $e \models PROG(T)$, then $e \models PERF(START(T))$.

Constraint 1, maximality, ensures that events are individuated, picking the largest chunk that supports the event-type. Constraint 2, the downward persistence of stickers, intuitively corresponds to the fact that any temporal part of a state of a certain type must be of that same type. This condition has been given various names in the literature, of which "homogeneity condition" and "downward closure" are most familiar. But note that the condition applies to stickers only, not to holes. Constraint 3 requires that the natural part-whole relation between types be preserved between events where such types are going on. This guarantees some of the inferences using part-whole relations between individuals that we discussed in chapter 2 for the monotonicity patterns with aspectual verbs. Constraint 4 requires that a perfect state be preceded by the event that caused it. Constraint 5 ensures that any part of an event of type T is one at which T is in progress, with the caveat, discussed before, that "in progress" means only that it has started and not yet ended or finished. In the event structures interruptions of ongoing actions are admitted, but the corresponding progressive stickers are supported throughout.

Constraint 6 requires a bit more discussion, for it ensures that the "imperfective paradox" is resolved. The puzzle is illustrated in (3.9).

(3.9)   a.   Jane was wandering around. $\Rightarrow$ Jane wandered around.
         b.   Jane was reading this book. $\nRightarrow$ Jane read this book.

Why is it that in (3.9a) we infer the simple past from a past progressive when the embedded type is a hole, whereas such an inference is invalid in (3.9b), where the embedded type is a filter?

Given the definition of situated entailment, a simple past tense conclusion cannot in general be a situated entailment from merely a progressive past premise. The literature on the "imperfective paradox" has primarily been concerned with static logical entailment based only on truth-conditions, often in a possible-worlds interval semantics.[15] Such approaches typically define the meaning of the progressive in terms of the meaning of its nonprogressive counterpart, appealing to notions of completions or culminations of the ongoing event, given certain closed-world assumptions. They disregard the fact that aspectual classes have a different role to play in dynamic updates of contexts, since they are not concerned with discourse representation. In the dynamic DAT representation, the meaning of the progressive is not truth-conditionally defined; instead, it is captured in the rule to represent progressives as stickers and its associated inference rules in (3.8). In a DAT the progressive premise of (3.9) is represented as a sticker on a given current node, and the nonprogressive conclusion should be added to the same node. But the only types for which this is intuitively valid are the holes, an observation that is simply guaranteed by constraint 6, admitting that this is just a special characteristic inherent to the way holes are used. Even though adopting this rule may seem to provide little explanatory insight into the reason why holes are used in such a particular way, the puzzle is accounted for in a very simple manner, on a par with the account of how we use other aspectual information. The modal accounts of the "imperfective paradox" are fraught with conceptual difficulties in explaining just how much variation to permit in the relevant inertia worlds while the event is continued, or how things might have been different in the past part of it, leading up to its actual stage. Interruptions are very natural in any long-term process or action—often even necessary to satisfy the presuppositions of continuing the action. Writing a book certainly requires interruptions; the writer must stop to rest, in order to be able to resume and ultimately finish the task. We ordinarily measure the duration of an event after its completion by gauging the time elapsed between its unique start and finish. When we interrupt our action at some arbitrary time, the result of our action rarely depends on the exact time at which it was interrupted. In having to explain just how an action must be structured in order to be considered "normal," issues of culture, causality, control, and social values are raised that a semantic theory should not have to answer.

The remaining three constraints in (3.8) are concerned with the internal structure of events: constraint 7 requires the obvious relation between precedence and starting point; constraint 8 ensures the relation between start-events and the aspectual verb *start*. Finally, constraint 9 simply requires that an event in progress must have been started—an assumption used in the inferences discussed.

A sequence of sentences or text is *interpretable* in an event structure iff there is an embedding of a DAT, constructed by the rules in an interpretation of this text, into that event structure. The text *describes* part of the event structure via the embedding of its DAT; this is defined in (3.10).

(3.10)   Let D be a DAT and f an embedding of it into an event structure. Then D *describes* f iff

for all nodes n in D and all types T
if T labels n in D, then $f(n) \models T$ in the event structure.

That part of the event structure providing values for the described embedding is called the *described episode*. A text is *true* just in case the episode the DAT describes is part of the world. A true text is called *factual;* a text that is interpretable, but not true, is called *fictional*. This allows for the possibility that interpretable texts may consist of factual and fictional parts.

The traditional notion of logical entailment is a static truth-preserving relation between the set of premises and the conclusion of an inference. But we now realize that the information obtained by interpreting the premises of an argument is about an entire episode, whereas the conclusion is concerned only with the final part of that episode corresponding to the current node. In reasoning with a DAT, the conclusion describes an event via the embedding of the current node of that DAT, which represents the information obtained by processing its premises. But each premise describes only part of the entire episode, terminating with the event described by the conclusion. To capture this context-dependence of temporal reasoning, the notion of situated entailment in DATs is now defined as in (3.11).

(3.11)   *Definition of situated entailment*
Let D be a DAT for the premises $T_1, \ldots, T_n$ and let c be its current node. Then $T_1, \ldots, T_n \vdash T$ iff for all event structures S and all embeddings f of D into S, if $T_1, \ldots, T_n$ describes $f(D)$, then $f(c)$ is of type T.

The DAT representations mix aspectual control information with descriptive information and perspectival information. Situated entailment is formalized as a relation between a DAT for a text, its current node, and its embeddings into event structures. Integrating such different kinds of information is required in representing the content of a text. Chapter 7 contains some further reflection on foundational issues of DAT representations, along with a discussion of the role of parametric types in modeling temporal reasoning.

Chapter 4
States, Generic Information, and Constraints

Stative information is always represented by a sticker on either the current node in a DAT, if it is a plug, or the one introduced next, if the current one is a hole; it never contributes a new node by itself. As we have already seen, the different forms in which stative information is expressed are represented by different stickers. Some stative information is of a more permanent nature than other stative information, for it is less volatile in context change and belongs to the core of stable constraints that we use to make sense of what we are interpreting. In DAT representations these differences between stickers are captured by associating various portability conditions with the stickers in perspectival shifts, when a new chronoscope is created. Stable information is easily imported into new chronoscopes, whereas highly context-sensitive stative information is very limited in its portability. The use we make of presuppositions and entailments in constructing DATs is again evident in designing the portability conditions for stickers.

4.1 Transient States

Although states do not have any internal temporal structure in the sense that events consist of beginning, middle, and terminal stages, some states may still be transient and temporary in the sense that their duration is limited. Their onset must be caused by events, and they terminate because an event causally interferes with them. In previous chapters we encountered various descriptions of such states, collected here in (4.1).

(4.1) a. Jane was happy.
       b. Jane felt ill.
       c. It was not even noon yet.
       d. She was now ready to call.

All examples of transient states in (4.1) are described in the simple past. These states must be represented by stickers appended to nodes that must satisfy the constraint associated with past tense: the node the stickers attach to must precede the source node of the DAT. Only if the DAT does not already contain such a current past node may the interpretation of past tense stative information have the dynamic effect of introducing such a node, a hole, to satisfy the global tense constraint. Such a dynamic effect of interpreting stative information was illustrated in figure 3.6. This dynamic effect is triggered in such cases by the past tense constraint—not by the sticker rule, for it never has any dynamic effect.

Simple transient states are often described in English by using the copula *be* or *have* (4.1a, c, d) or verbs describing mental states (4.1b). Like descriptions of events, they can be constrained by the indexical adverb *now* (4.1d), referring to the event to which the node at which the corresponding sticker is attached is mapped by embedding the DAT into an event structure. Simple states also show negative polarity effects triggered by adverbs like *not yet* in (4.1c).

Stative information expressed in linguistic descriptions of such transient states is characteristically true throughout the state (i.e., at any arbitrary point within the state). In chapter 3 this characteristic logical behavior of stickers was captured by the semantic constraint 2 on event structures in (3.8), which requires the downward persistence of stickers in any part of a situation that supports a sticker. In the syntactic terms of DAT representation this means that the sticker may be copied freely to any node it dominates, so the stative information is shared by the different chronoscopes that include the node at which the sticker was introduced. As a consequence, if a sticker labels a node in the current chronoscope, it can be derived as a situated consequence at the current node and reported using the simple past. None of the types that label nodes introduced by the interpretation may ever be transmitted to other nodes. This downward portability of stickers applies to all the different kinds of stickers. In chapter 6 the mental attitude verbs and the auxiliary verbs *be* and *have* are encoded in the lexicon with a left-down arrow, representing, in their restrictor or context, their aspectual force of preserving the current chronoscope.[1] Downward portability is captured here as a specific constraint on DATs, expressed as a simple copying operation on a DAT.

(4.2)   *Downward portability of stickers*
If a node n is labeled with a sticker in any given DAT, copy the sticker freely to the labels of all nodes n dominates.

Portability conditions on stickers are formulated entirely in terms of configurational relations between nodes in DATs. They are related to the semantic constraints formulated in (3.8) as rules of proof in a logical system are related to semantic inference rules. If the properties of this system of DAT representation were studied abstractly as a temporal logic, the nature of the relation between the portability conditions on stickers and the relevant semantic constraints would have to be provably sound and complete. However, it is beyond the scope of this book to show this, since its focus is primarily on the empirical linguistic considerations and the design of DAT representations for ordinary English.

Can stickers ever be transmitted upward in a chronoscope? In its most general form, this question must be answered negatively. But we can characterize very specific conditions under which certain stickers can be imported into other chronoscopes. Transient states ordinarily last until something happens that causally interferes with them. This principle is implicitly assumed in our interpretations of narrative texts. For instance, in (4.3) the second clause describes a transient state, which in the DAT is appended as sticker to the plug representing Jane's arrival at the hospital. The third clause in (4.3) entails that Jane is still feeling ill, serving as explanatory background for why a doctor came to see her.

(4.3)   Jane arrived at the hospital. She felt very ill. A doctor came to see her.

Presupposing or entailing sticker information is a typical mechanism to ensure cohesion in a narrative text. But for a proper formulation of this interpretive principle, we need to understand in what sense the three clauses in (4.3) provide information about the same topic, introduced by the first sentence. In this case it is perhaps easy to identify the topic preservation because of the anaphoric chain of coreference to Jane. But coreference is not generally required to preserve a topic the information is about, as illustrated in (4.4), which similarly preserves the topic introduced by the first clause.

(4.4)   Jane arrived at the hospital. The cramps were unbearable now. There was no one at the desk.

For our present, more limited concerns of temporal reasoning, a general principle can be formulated to the effect that presupposed or entailed stative information in stickers may be imported to the label of a node by accommodation, even if the nodes are in different chronoscopes. More global coherence conditions, commonsense knowledge, and principles of discourse structure should constrain this principle of accommodation sufficiently to prohibit copying stickers over to chronoscopes after information is given that the state no longer holds. In any case, a closure condition should ensure that the lowest node dominating two nodes with the same sticker should also carry that sticker. This creates a rather constrained upward portability effect for stickers, based on accommodation. The two principles are formulated in (4.5) as DAT operations.

(4.5)   *Portability conditions for accommodation*
In any given DAT, if a sticker S labels a node n in chronoscope C and if a node m in a chronoscope C', where n precedes m, presupposes or entails S, then

i.   Copy S to m.
ii. Closure condition
     Copy S to the lowest node that C and C' share.

Again, the principle in (4.5) still needs further constraining by some discourse rules or inferential principles from other domains, but I will not attempt to formulate such principles here. Note also that the general DAT requirement that the information carried on the nodes of a given chronoscope be compatible is still in force.

4.2 Progressive and Perfect States

Other descriptions of states have a more complex linguistic structure. There are two kinds: progressives and perfects. As was illustrated in chapter 3, the markers for progressive and perfect in the aspectual component of Infl in the syntax are represented in the types by *PROG* and *PERF*. Both describe stative relations between the node and the event of the embedded type: the progressive requires the node to represent a temporal part of that event, and the perfect requires the current node to be preceded by a node in some chronoscope labeled with that type. If the fragment included future or modal auxiliary verbs, it would complete this picture by requiring the node labeled with a future/modal sticker to precede a node in some later chronoscope representing the event of the embedded type. We presuppose that progressive states must already have started and not yet have ended at the current node. Of course, anything that is currently going on may sometime come to an end, but it may also never end. There is no need for a semantic theory to characterize what it takes for an action to reach completion, for it all depends on the kind of action, on the plans and intentions of its participants, and in fact on a host of external factors that may causally affect the described action. The semantic and logical characteristics of the use of the progressive are determined by their representation as stickers and by the associated presuppositions.

Perfect states are caused by the ending of the event supporting the embedded type. So they begin at the point where the causing event ends, but they themselves never end, no matter what happens later. Some descriptions of transient states entail descriptions of perfect states, as in (4.6).

(4.6)   Jane was at the hospital. $\Rightarrow$ Jane had arrived at the hospital.

But if at a later time Jane left the hospital, we infer at that time that she is no longer at the hospital, although she (once) had arrived there. Since perfect states last forever, stickers that describe them are easily imported into later chronoscopes. It is obvious that stickers representing perfect states cannot be imported into the chronoscope of the node carrying the embedded type in its label, if that node represented the event causing the perfect state. If, however, the type is supported by another event, constituting another occurrence of the same type, there is no such restriction. For instance, when Jane arrives at the hospital again, she must already have arrived there before. This restricts the portability of perfect stickers to the domain containing all the right-sister nodes of any node in the chronoscope that contains the node representing the event that caused the perfect state, as captured in constraint 1 of (4.7). If information about the event that caused the perfect state is lacking, the portability of the sticker is restricted to the domain dominated by its right-sister node, which in linguistic, configurational terms is called its *c-command domain*, as captured in constraint 2 of (4.7).

(4.7)   *Portability constraint on PERF stickers*
1.   In any given DAT, if a node n is labeled with a sticker $PERF(T)$ in chronoscope C, and a node m is labeled with T in an earlier chronoscope C', then this sticker is imported in C to nodes preceded and dominated by C'.
2.   In any given DAT, if a node n is labeled with a sticker $PERF(T)$ in chronoscope C, and no node m is labeled with T in an earlier chronoscope C', then this sticker is imported into the c-command domain of n.

For progressive stickers, the situation is more complicated. If all we know is that something is going on, ordinarily we do not know whether it will stop or end, unless the action is under our own control. But if the DAT already contains information that the action has ended, some node in the chronoscope containing the node labeled with the $PROG(T)$ represents the event of type T. Only in that configuration may the $PROG$ sticker be transmitted upward in the chronoscope to the nodes dominated by the node labeled T. The portability of progressive stickers is captured in (4.8).

(4.8)   *Portability condition on PROG stickers*
In any given DAT, if a node n is labeled with a type T in the chronoscope C and the sticker $PROG(T)$ labels a dependent node m, then the sticker $PROG(T)$ may be copied to any node that n dominates in C.

The constraint in (4.8) corresponds to the procedure discussed in chapter 3 to verify a progressive conclusion: the embedding of the current node is of type $PROG(T)$, if (1) an ancestor node in the current chronoscope is labeled T or if (2) a left chronoscope contains a node labeled «*START*, T, $+$» and no intervening chronoscope contains a node labeled «*END*, T, $+$» or «*FINISH*, T, $+$».

The stickers representing perfect and progressive clauses have limited upward portability, constrained by (4.7) and (4.8). Of course, the general condition on downward portability in (4.2) and the condition on portability by accommodation in (4.5) also apply to them.

When a text opens with a number of consecutive clauses giving stative information as general background to the episode described by it, the stickers representing this information form an ordered list at the same node. In transmitting stickers to other nodes, this order should be preserved, for we use this textual order in our reasoning. Of course, when backing up in the given chronoscope, one collects the portable stickers, but each sticker must be checked for its compatibility with the new information. The new information may entail or presuppose that the transient state described by a sticker in the given chronoscope has ended. In such cases, the sticker that is incompatible with the new information drops out of the list and is not transmitted to the new chronoscope. This is a consequence of the general rule on maintaining compatible information within a chronoscope.

Listing stickers representing progressive or perfect information allows us to reason about the temporal relations between the events supporting their embedded types. The examples in (4.9)–(4.11) illustrate certain properties of the interaction of stickers in a list.

(4.9)   Jane strolled through the dark alleys. She wore her leather bomber and her hair was all tangled. She had bought what she needed. She arrived at the coffee shop.

(4.10)   Jane wore her leather bomber and her hair was all tangled. She strolled through the dark alleys. She had bought what she needed. She arrived at the coffee shop.

(4.11)   Jane wore her leather bomber and her hair was all tangled. She was strolling through the dark alleys. She had bought what she needed. She arrived at the coffee shop.

The DAT for (4.9) has a past chronoscope consisting of a hole (*stroll*), a dependent hole (*wear*), and a dependent plug (*arrive*) with the list of the two stickers $\langle$(*tangle*), (*PERF buy*)$\rangle$. But for (4.10) the chronoscope consists of a hole (*wear*), a dependent hole (*stroll*) with a sticker (*tangle*), and a dependent plug (*arrive*) with a sticker (*PERF buy*). The DAT for (4.11) consists of a hole (*wear*) and a dependent plug (*arrive*) with a list of three stickers $\langle$(*tangle*), (*PROG stroll*), (*PERF buy*)$\rangle$. The relevant sections of the three DATs are

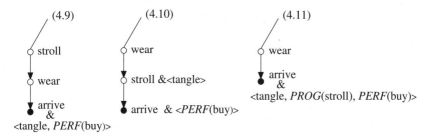

Figure 4.1
Partial DATs for (4.9), (4.10), and (4.11)

shown in figure 4.1 with abbreviated labels and the lists of stickers in angled brackets.

These three DATs show that the textual order in which stative information is given matters considerably to the way the DAT is constructed.[2] Given these DATs, can we make any situated inferences about when Jane bought what she needed and when she was strolling around? From all three DATs we infer that she *must* have bought what she needed before she arrived at the coffee shop and that she *may* or *may not* have bought it during her stroll. From (4.9) and (4.11) we infer that if she bought it on her stroll, her hair may, but need not, have been tangled. But only from (4.10) does it follow that, if she bought it on her stroll, her hair *must* have been tangled. Note that in both cases the inference about the state of her hair is conditional upon her having bought what she needed on her stroll. The information given in these three texts does not tell us whether this is in fact the case. This illustrates how situated inferences are used to reason conditionally with partial information, when the information given leaves open what is in fact the case. The first rule at work here is constraint 4 in (3.8): the perfect sticker $PERF(T)$ labeling node c implies that T must label a node in some chronoscope before c. When the list of stickers labeling c contains both a $PROG(T')$ sticker and $PERF(T)$, or when T' labels a node dominating c, we cannot infer anything about the temporal relation between events described by the two embedded types T and T'. This rule is also at work in the following example:

(4.12)   She was dialing. Her wallet had dropped on the ground.

From (4.12), can we conclude anything at all about the temporal relation between her wallet dropping and her dialing? Must the wallet have dropped before she started to dial, or after? We cannot tell from (4.12)— either is possible. But her wallet must have dropped before now, that is, before the point when she is dialing. If we change the order of these $PROG$ and $PERF$ stickers, we see the same inferential effects.

(4.13)   Her wallet had dropped on the ground. She was dialing.

Did the wallet drop before she started to dial? Again we cannot say anything about the temporal relation between her starting to dial and the time
her wallet dropped. Both have definitely happened in the past, but we
don't know in what order they or their constituent temporal parts in fact
happened. Using a progressive and a perfect cancels the dynamic effect of
the embedded type, and hence (4.9) and (4.11) allow for the same inferences despite the differences in the order in which the information was
given, all represented within the same chronoscope.[3] This illustration dem-
onstrates an important aspect of the interaction among holes introduced by
simple past clauses, simple stickers, *PROG* stickers, and *PERF* stickers. It
provides an important restriction on how we reason with lists of stickers
and illustrates again the significance of chronoscopes as structured temporal objects.

4.3 Generic Information

Besides describing transient, ongoing, or perfect states, we express stative
information about abstract objects like kinds or substances, describing
conditional or default connections between their properties or attributing
atemporal properties to them. Such information is typically used in explanatory reasoning and often is expressed in "analytic" statements, considered
true irrespective of context, because of the meaning of their descriptive
vocabulary.

An important distinction is made in the current literature on generics
between *characteristic-kind predication*, in which a property is attributed under default "normality" assumptions to all members of the kind, and *proper-
kind predication*, which attributes a property to the kind that cannot be
attributed to any of its members.[4] The former, but not the latter, admits of
exceptions to the correlation that is established, as illustrated in (4.14a) and
(4.14b), respectively.

(4.14)   a.   Public phones are often coin-operated.
          b.   A public phone is rarely in working order.

In (4.14a) the clause describes a regular correlation between the property of
being a public phone and the property of being operated by coins. Such a
regularity remains true even in situations where there are no public phones
or where all of the existing public phones are out of order. Even when
some new model of public phone has been introduced that operates by
phone cards, we use (4.14a) to describe the regularity. In (4.14b) the property of being rare is attributed to the public phones in working order, not
to any individual public phone. Obviously there are various meaningful

connections between the two ways of expressing generic information that may play a role in our reasoning with such information.[5] Here we will focus on the proper representation of these two forms of generic information in DATs.

Arguments of relations in types labeling nodes in a DAT may be mapped onto kinds by embedding them into event structures. We refer demonstratively to a kind—for instance, exclaiming in a phone booth *There isn't any room in these phone booths!* Not only do we describe the lack of space in the particular phone booth we are in, but we claim simultaneously, on the supposition that other phone booths are constructed just like it, that this model phone booth lacks sufficient room. Phone booths that are not similar to the one we are in are excluded from our consideration, as are phone booths that are similar in the relevant respects but fail some other default assumption in the background. For instance, a phone booth just like the one we are in, from which the phone was stolen, may constitute another type of exception. Such demonstrative reference to kinds not only relies on the similarity relations fixed by the actual member of the kind one is given information about but also requires preservation of the background conditions, including other generic information, either assumed, presupposed, or explicitly asserted, and possibly further conditional correlations between properties of the kind.

In DAT representations, generic information is stative and hence represented by means of stickers. Such generic stickers are the only ones freely imported to the root of the DAT, if no information incompatible with their restrictor is encountered. In this way the generic information they encode is preserved throughout the different chronoscopes that arise in the interpretation of a text.

(4.15)   *Portability constraint on generic stickers*
In any given DAT generic stickers are freely imported upward, as long as their restrictor is supported.

A generic sticker representing a proper-kind predication must contain a parameter as a verbal argument that refers to a kind. When the clause represents a characteristic-kind predication, the sticker has as its main relation a default relation *GEN* between two roles, abstracted from the types, respectively called the *restrictor* and its *nuclear scope*.

$$«[x_1, \ldots, x_n | T] \; GEN \; [x_1, \ldots, x_n, \; y_1, \ldots, y_n | T']».$$

Ordinarily the subject NP of a characteristic-kind predication is represented in the restrictor, together with other types of situational or background information, and the remaining VP is represented in the nuclear scope. This is a rule of thumb in mapping English clauses to types, which has a number of well-known restrictions partly induced by prosodic information or the nature of the predicates used.[6]

The embedding of nodes labeled with these *GEN* stickers into situations that support them is defined as follows. The restrictor constrains the type of situation about which the generic information is given.

(4.16)   *Semantics of GEN stickers*
Let f be an embedding of a DAT with a node n into an event structure. Then

$$f(n) \models «[x_1, \ldots, x_n | T] \; GEN \; [x_1, \ldots, x_n, y_1, \ldots, y_n | T']»$$

iff every proper extension g of f such that
i. $g(n') \models T$ and
ii. $g(n')$ is at least as similar to $f(n)$ as any other $g'(n') \models T$
can be extended to $h(n') \models T'$.

Clause (ii) in (4.16) requires the extensions g of f that support the restrictor to preserve most similarity conditions determined for T at $f(n)$. Although generic information is supported in a situation that itself need not satisfy the restrictor, it requires the situations that do support the restrictor to support the nuclear scope. This ensures that any differences in the situations that support the restrictor of the generic sticker are irrelevant to the kind about which the generic information is expressed. For example, a situation containing a phone booth of which the glass wall has been shattered may still support the generic information that there is no room in such phone booths. But the situation itself constitutes an exception, since it does not preserve the relevant similarity relations with the phone booth in which this clause was uttered. This means also that the phone booth with a shattered glass wall itself cannot itself serve as a proper situation to anchor the demonstrative *these phone booths*. The preservation of background conditions is regulated by the general principles of DAT representation and the requirement of maintaining compatible information in a chronoscope. In particular, generic information expressed by proper-kind predication is typically preserved throughout the entire interpretation, because the stickers representing such information have no restrictor and can be transmitted to the root. Hence, such stickers are the most independent of the node at which they were introduced.

4.4 *Conditionals and Temporal Quantification*

Stative information can also be expressed in the form of conditionals and quantifying adverbial clauses. These forms of expressing stative information are illustrated in (4.17).[7]

(4.17)   a.   If Jane called back, she needed a coin.
         b.   Whenever Jane called back, she needed a coin.

Both conditional and adverbially quantified clauses are represented in complex types appended according to the sticker rule to the current or next node in a DAT. The difference between a pure conditional connection between two clauses and the temporal adverbial connection is manifested in the way they constrain generic information. In general, as illustrated in (4.18), conditional antecedents modify the given context to set the conditions for the interpretation of its consequent clause, whereas temporal adverbial clauses contribute conditions to the generic information restricting what kind information is given about.

(4.18)   a.   When public phones were coin-operated, they were
              used a lot.
         b.   If public phones were coin-operated, they were used a
              lot.

In (4.18a) it is asserted that at the time the public phones were coin-operated, they were used a lot. This is generic information about public phones at the time they were coin-operated, represented by a *GEN* sticker whose restrictor contains the public phones in the past. At the very least (4.18a) invites the contrastive inference that public phones are no longer coin-operated and perhaps consequently used less often. But this is only a pragmatic implicature, since it may be canceled by continuing with the assertion that in fact the ones that are still coin-operated are used a lot, exploiting a causal link between their being coin-operated and their being frequently used. In (4.18b) it is asserted that in the past coin-operated public phones were used a lot. This excludes from consideration the card-operated public phones that existed in the past, and no inference is invited that they were used any less. The conditional antecedent contributes a general condition to the given context, so that it asserts that the coin-operated public phones were used a lot then, typically uttered with a high pitch contour on *coin-operated*.[8] In other words, as opposed to the temporal quantification in (4.18a), the pure conditional in (4.18b) does not tell us anything about the present public phones, coin-operated or not. It should be represented by a *GEN* sticker representing the generic connection in the past between those public phones that were coin-operated and their frequent use. Other situations supporting the similarity conditions incorporated in this *GEN* sticker must preserve the background condition that some public phones were coin-operated in the past.

In general, pure conditionals do not provide additional restrictions on the kind described by characteristic-kind-predication statements, whereas quantifying temporal adverbs like *when* and *whenever* do. But if the conditional correlation is strengthened to be understood as a causal correlation, and the antecedent describes the cause of the event described by the consequent, this difference between conditionals and temporally quantifying adverbs is obliterated. This is illustrated in (4.19), assuming that vandalizing a phone makes it useless.

(4.19) a. Public phones are useless when they are vandalized.
        b. Public phones are useless if they are vandalized.
        c. Vandalized public phones are useless.

Both the conditional in (4.19b) and the temporally quantified antecedent in (4.19a) describe what makes a public phone useless. Their content is equivalent to the generic information about vandalized public phones expressed in the simple characteristic-kind predication in (4.19c). The *ceteris paribus* condition associated with causal laws serves to stabilize the background conditions and relegates cases that do not follow the law to the status of exceptions.[9]

It is interesting to note that reasons as opposed to causes do not suffice to strengthen the correlation described by the conditional. This is illustrated in (4.20), assuming that the cash in the phone causes someone to break into it, as opposed to the weaker correlation where petty thieves have a reason to try their luck with coin-operated phones because they may contain cash.

(4.20) a. When a public phone contains cash, it is broken into.
        b. Public phones are broken into, when they contain cash.
        c. Cash-containing public phones are broken into.
        d. If a public phone is coin-operated, it is broken into.
        e. Public phones are broken into, if they are
            coin-operated.
        f. Coin-operated public phones are broken into.

In (4.20a–c) the same generic information about phones with cash is expressed in three different forms. The conditional of (4.20d) expresses the stronger information that all public phones are broken into, because they are coin-operated and hence may contain cash. One can imagine that a manufacturer of card-operated public phones, eager to make a sale, would use (4.20d, e, or f) to paint a bleak picture asserting generically about coin-operated public phones that they all get broken into, not just the ones that actually have been seen in use and hence are certain to contain cash. Using (4.20e) focuses attention on a generic aspect of coin-operated phones, which may also be expressed as the simple characteristic-kind predication in (4.20f). Much more of semantic interest remains to be analyzed regarding the interaction between *when* clauses and conditionals and the way various forms of generic information is expressed. An especially interesting issue is how prosodic information may give clues about what information is considered part of the restrictor and what information is not. This may in fact overrule the general principle that only the subject NP in characteristic-kind predications is contained in the restrictor. But such issues extend much beyond our present concern with temporal reasoning and the representation of tense and aspect in DATs.

Chapter 5

Perspectives

Wir werden uns des Aspekts nur im Wechsel bewusst. Wie wenn sich Einer nur des Wechselns der Tonart bewusst ist, aber kein absolutes Gehör hat.
Ludwig Wittgenstein

Reasoning about time employs various forms of situated inference, as the preceding chapters have shown. The information used in such reasoning depends simultaneously on the source issuing the information and on the event currently described, represented in DATs by distinct nodes. The information represented in a DAT gives a certain perspective on the episode it describes. This notion of a *perspective* forms the central topic of this chapter.[1]

A DAT constitutes a perspective on the described episode via its embedding into events supporting the types that label its nodes in an event structure. Different DATs resulting from the interpretation of one text may describe the same episode but offer different perspectives on it. Since the configurational structure of a DAT determines what situated conclusions can be inferred from the information it represents, different perspectives on the same episode not only provide different information about what happened, but also allow different conclusions. If a DAT is updated by the hole rule or the sticker rule, the information is added within the same perspective. But if a DAT is updated by the plug rule or the filler rule, which back up to a higher node in the current chronoscope, the perspective is shifted because a new chronoscope is created. Coherence and consistency of the information gathered in the interpretation are ensured by creating properly constrained perspectival shifts, according to the rules for DAT construction in chapter 3 together with the portability conditions associated with the stickers as defined in section 5.1. Perspectives may also be refined in a narrative flashback, when the text redirects the current node to add new information within an already closed chronoscope in a DAT. Such updating of DATs by refining the perspective is rather constrained, as argued in section 5.2. Perspectival refinement constitutes an interesting semantic process, since it may also constrain the availability of NP antecedents to bind subsequent occurrences of pronouns after the flashback.

If perspectival refinement is included as a general operation on DATs, we no longer need to define filters as offering an interpretive choice between holes and plugs. Instead, a filter is always represented as a plug, but perspectival refinement may "unplug" it and turn it into a hole, if the new information meets certain well-defined conditions. This makes the interpretation algorithm within the semantic theory deterministic, in the sense that any text is interpreted by a finite number of DATs. In constructing a DAT, an interpreter makes decisions only about which external constraints from other domains to use in his reasoning. Semantic theory offers little guidance in deciding whether a text admits of a causal interpretation or not. But if the interpreter decides to use a causal constraint in his interpretation, the semantic representation incorporates it and spells out the consequences. In 5.3 we will consider how information issuing from multiple sources may be integrated into richer DAT representations, describing scenes and scenarios.

5.1 Perspectival Coherence and Chronoscopes

Any DAT, with its designated current node in the current chronoscope, and its unique root and source, determines a *perspective* on the described situation or episode. The given perspective is preserved as long as the newly introduced nodes extend the current chronoscope. In other words, holes preserve the perspective by extending the current chronoscope; plugs trigger shifts of perspective. If an interpretation is formalized as a sequence of DATs, as in chapter 3, certain sections of such a sequence determine the same perspective, if they are created by the chronoscope-preserving hole rule or sticker rule. Hence, different DATs may determine the same perspective, even though they contain different information and different current nodes.

Shifting the perspective of a DAT is a procedure that may be composed of various actions. When the current node c in the given chronoscope is a plug, the interpretation must create a new chronoscope. Ordinarily the plug rule simply introduces a right sister to the current node and sets it to be the new current node. But if the new information is incompatible with some information contained in the current chronoscope, a more complex procedure is needed. First, the interpretation backs up in the current chronoscope to the hole nearest to c that is labeled with an incompatible type. This hole is plugged up, by closing its internal structure, and it is selected as the current node. Now the plug rule is applied to it. Accordingly, a new node is introduced as its right sister, labeled with the type representing the new information and sharing the stickers on its parent node. Creating a new chronoscope by shifting the perspective in a DAT ordinarily ensures that the given and new chronoscopes have at least one node in common; that is, the root must at least be preserved in perspectival shifts as background information.

The shifting of the perspective during the interpretation of a text not only maintains compatible information encoded in the labels of the nodes in the same chronoscope but also requires that all the information contained in the DAT be *coherent*. Coherence of information is a notoriously slippery concept, for it requires a better understanding of what topics are that speakers give information about and how speakers signal a change of topic. Although this book does not attempt to answer such issues, some aspects of coherence of information can be made more precise in the context of DAT representation. Disregarding the complexities of perspectival refinement momentarily, recall that new chronoscopes always introduce a new nodes as a *right* sister to the current node in the current chronoscope.[2] The rules for DAT construction guarantee right branching, which captures an essential aspect of coherence of the information within a DAT. The method by which information is expressed in natural-language narrative texts does not admit left branching in DATs, nor can the interpretation insert new branches between existing ones. But coherence of the information contained in a DAT requires more. First, any DAT requires that the information be issued from a unique source. Second, its root should be shared by all the chronoscopes arising in the interpretation. In other words, a perspectival shift that would introduce a sister node to the root violates its internal coherence. These basic requirements on coherence of information in a DAT are captured as a constraint, formulated in (5.1) as a relation between perspectives.

(5.1)   *Coherence of perspectives*
Let P and P' be two perspectives determined by DATs D and D', respectively. Then P is *coherent* with P' iff

i. D' is obtained from D by applying the rules for DAT construction and portability constraints,

ii.   the root of D is the root of D' (modulo additional stickers),

iii. the source of D is the source of D'.

Introducing a right sister to the given root is still an admissible move in DAT construction, since the construction rules do not require that we add only nodes dependent upon the same root. But the perspective so created would not be coherent with the given one, according to (5.1). Such an update violates the coherence of the information contained in a DAT. This seems justified as long as we are primarily interested in temporal reasoning about the past and wish to avoid a host of complications induced by the

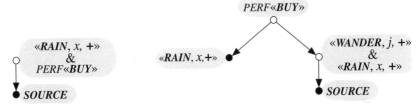

Figure 5.1
Uprooting a DAT

interpretation of present tense. But if present tense were to be included, some quite natural narratives would allow the introduction of a new root to maintain coherence. For example, suppose the root in the DAT given in figure 5.1 contains the information about the present that it is raining, represented by a simple sticker, and the information that Jane has bought a bomber jacket, represented by a *PERF* sticker.[3] Now we get new information that it is no longer raining and that Jane wanders through a sleazy neighborhood. Using the filler rule to back up to the lowest node carrying compatible information, we must plug up the root, because it carries the label representing the fact that it is raining. Introducing a right sister to it would require first creating a new root to serve as common parent to the given root, the new current node, and the source node. This root is introduced with no label, at least for the time being. The information that Jane wanders through a sleazy neighborhood introduces a new hole to be the current node, referring to a new present event. Although unlabeled nodes were not explicitly ruled out in the original syntactic conditions on DATs in chapter 3, allowing them could easily lead to uncontrolled growth of empty nodes. This would not constitute a sound representational practice, for unlabeled nodes are supported by anything. A node without a label lacks the descriptive information that gives proper constitutive content to the embedding of that node into the event structure.[4] Fortunately, in this particular example the label of the new root is filled, since the portability conditions on the PERF sticker attached to the former root allow it to be transmitted to the new root. Coherence is rescued after all by applying the portability constraints for the stickers in the DAT in this case. Of course, the source node needs another kind of operation in present tense narratives, for it must remain dominated by the current node in any perspectival shift, as required by the general conditions on DATs.

From this example the following additional rule for DAT construction and constraints may now be formulated for fragments that include present tense:

(5.2)   *Root rule*
If the root is plugged up in an application of the filler rule, introduce a new hole as the new root, parent to the given root, the source node, and the new current node.

(5.3)   *Constraint on label assignment*
The function α_N from N to the powerset of *TYPE* assigns each node in a DAT a *nonempty* set of types.

If the constraint (5.3) is violated, the label of the new root remains empty after "uprooting" (as applications of the root rule are called informally), because no stickers are transmitted to it. In this case the perspectival shift breaks down the coherence of the information. This means that there is no common background information, so the new perspective initiates a new story line. Similar breakdowns of coherence may be caused by resetting the source issuing the information.

Clause (ii) in the definition (5.1) of coherence as a relation between perspectives should now be amended to allow for such uprooting.

(5.4)   *Amendment to (5.1)*
ii.   The root of D is the root of D' (modulo additional stickers) or the root of D is a child of the root of D' (modulo additional stickers).

Uprooting a DAT violates the coherence of the information within its perspective only if it results in an unlabeled node. If no background information can be preserved by importing stickers into the new chronoscope, there is no continuing story line. Perhaps the new story will provide some stickers later that can be transmitted to the new root, which would integrate the prior story and the new one. But such high-level forms of integrating information are presently beyond the intended scope of the system of DAT representations.

The notion of a chronoscope was defined as the set of labeled nodes connected by arrows that starts at the root of any DAT and ends at one of its terminal nodes. Chronoscopes already have proven their value in characterizing the portability conditions on stickers, defining systematic verification procedures, and characterizing various valid forms of situated temporal reasoning on DATs. Chronoscopes have also turned out to be useful in defining coherence as a relation between perspectives. Furthermore, they are needed in the interpretation of the temporal indexicals and demonstratives *now, then, later,* and *earlier.*

In chapter 2 the aspectual verbs were interpreted as describing relations between a contextually determined reference time c and the event-type E representing the informative content of the complement clause. Instead of appealing to the external notion of a reference time, the restrictor of an aspectual verb is now better considered to be the entire chronoscope in a DAT. All information in the current chronoscope serves as context or background in which the descriptive type is interpreted. This provides a natural link between the kinematics of the left arrows and the rules of DAT representation. Left-up arrows are associated in the lexicon with the actions in the top of the cube. In English they are expressed with the existential aspectual verbs *start, stop, finish,* and *resume,* classified as plugs. They provide the control information, shifting the perspective, to back up in the given chronoscope to create a new chronoscope. Left-down arrows are associated in the lexicon with the actions in the bottom of the cube. They are expressed in English with the quantificational aspectual verbs *continue* and *keep* and the stative *end,* which presupposes that the action has already been stopped. The left-down arrows correspond to holes, letting the new information through, extending the current chronoscope downward. This preserves the given reference of the demonstrative and deictic temporal expressions and hence preserves the given perspective, although information is added and the DAT is updated.

5.2 *Perspectival Refinement*

To escape from the physical limitations that result in the linearity of narratives, natural languages contain various means to add information about an event already described, represented by a node in a previous chronoscope. In literary analysis this process is called a *flashback.* In this section the DAT rules are enriched with new rules to allow for this process, here called *perspectival refinement,* constrained by specific conditions on the operations. When we supply additional information about events we have described before, this may be marked by specific linguistic means, but it need not be overtly signaled. Often we must infer that new information describes an event we have already heard about.

Let us first examine some examples of such flashbacks and discuss how they can be represented in DATs.

(5.5) a. Jane called the number. Her wallet fell on the floor. There was no answer, so she hung up. She left the phone booth.

b. She had heard a loud scream across the canal, when she started to call. Someone was getting hurt badly. She decided to take a look.

c. She had heard a loud scream across the canal, as she was calling. Someone was getting hurt badly. She decided to take a look.

d.   As she was calling the number, she had heard a loud scream across the canal. Someone had gotten hurt badly. She decided to take a look.

e.   Before she had finished her call, she had heard a loud scream across the canal. Someone was getting hurt badly. She decided to take a look.

f.   When the phone was ringing, she had heard a loud scream across the canal. Someone got hurt badly. She decided to take a look.

When we continue the story in (5.5a) with (5.5b), the *when* adverb and the simple past existential aspectual verb *start* together require a new node dominated by the *call* node described in the first clause of (5.5a).[5] The chronoscope containing the node representing this calling event precedes the current chronoscope at this point in the DAT construction. The plug representing Jane's hanging up redirected the interpretation and created the current chronoscope containing her leaving the phone booth, represented by a node that is right sister to the *call* node. The DAT for the text in (5.5a) is given with abbreviated labels in figure 5.2. In order to incorporate the information in (5.5b) into this DAT, the interpreter must reset the current node to the calling event, and unplug it temporarily to make it the current chronoscope that can represent the information expressed in the simple past in (5.5b). But this flashback is facilitated by the fact that the first clause uses the past perfect, *she had heard . . .*, which is a sticker at the *leave* node. Using the semantic constraint 4 for perfect stickers and the new *when*-clause information, the interpreter now locates the event that caused the perfect state within the event of Jane's calling. The new, inferred information about her hearing the scream must be represented as dependent on the calling event. The flashback redirects the perspective to the chronoscope containing the call and resets it to be the current node. But the flashback information does not give any clue about how it should be related to the information that is already represented in the DAT in the nodes dependent on the *call* node. We do not know whether Jane heard the scream at the

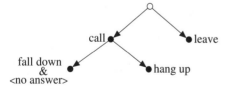

Figure 5.2
DAT for (5.5a)

moment her wallet fell down, which also occurred during her call. So the existing nodes dominated by the *call* node should not interact with the nodes introduced by the flashback information. Of course, within (5.5b) itself the DAT rules apply again, taking the start node to be the current node. The past progressive clause *was getting hurt* is a sticker on the start node. But did Jane decide to take a look then, or did she decide after she left the phone booth? The information given does not determine where the *decide* node, a plug, should be. Perhaps later information presupposes that Jane is still in the phone booth, which would supply the right information to disambiguate this. But the interpreter at this point is forced to maintain two DATs as possible interpretations. One DAT puts the decision after leaving the phone booth, resetting the perspective to the main one from which the flashback was created. The other maintains the flashback and adds the *decide* plug as dependent on the *call* node. Inferential relations may connect nodes introduced in the flashback to the ones introduced earlier in the main text, as long as they are independent of the node to which the flashback information is added. For instance, we do infer in both DATs that Jane must have heard the scream before she left the phone booth.

The process of perspectival refinement requires three new operations on DATs: (1) to unplug nodes in old chronoscopes, (2) to reset the current node to an old one, and (3) to allow for independence between the existing nodes and the newly added ones dominated by the same ancestor.

When we continue the narrative in (5.5a) with (5.5c) instead of (5.5b), the same flashback effect is observed. The perfect *had heard* triggers the semantic constraint again, which introduces the *hear* node below the *call* node. The temporal adverb *as*, together with the progressive *was calling*, apparently also triggers the perspectival refinement. Of course, that Jane had started to call is an entailment at the current node of the first clause in (5.5c), so the unplugging of the *call* node may be supported as well by the accommodation of this information. The simple past *decided* in the next clause again leaves open whether it is included in the flashback or not.

If we instead continue (5.5a) with (5.5d), the perfect clauses are represented as stickers on the *call* node. Now we cannot infer that Jane heard the scream during her call. The information presented in perfect clauses does not trigger a flashback, even if the descriptive verb initiating the flashback is in the simple past, as *call* is in (5.5d). By comparison, (5.5e) contains a perfect clause as well, but it also contains an existential aspectual verb, *finish*. It describes the completion of Jane's call, which presupposes her having started it and (again by reasoning with the semantic constraint 4) requires its node to be dominated by the *call* node. Accommodation of the presupposition triggers the flashback, since we can now continue with a simple past describing what happened during the call.

If we instead continue (5.5a) with a perfect clause as in (5.5f), added as a sticker to the current node (the *leave* node), the subsequent clause with the simple past *Someone got hurt badly* introduces a new node that is sister to it. This leads to an odd result, unless some special interpretive resources are applied. The perspective has not been refined by the perfect clause, since it merely introduced a sticker onto the *leave* node. The use of the semantic constraint 4 to locate the cause of the perfect state must be supported by asserted or presupposed simple past clauses to trigger a flashback. The mere inferred information that some past chronoscope contained the cause does not itself suffice. The situated information contained in simple past descriptions of events is the actual trigger of a flashback. In such an odd context, the interpreter sometimes reverts to a special strategy. The simple past is interpreted as a description of what Jane thought, when she heard the loud scream, and presumably still thinks, allowing the simple past as sticker representing her thought, a mental state. The descriptive information is in this case interpreted as if it were embedded under a main mental-attitude verb, describing Jane's "interior monologue" at the time she heard the scream. But such special interpretive strategies quickly lead into issues that border on the literary. Flashback effects and just what triggers them in narratives raise very important and interesting questions for natural-language semanticists concerned with informational structure and representational architecture. It is important to allow DATs to incorporate such information about old nodes by formulating new rules for perspectival refinement.

Perspectival refinement is a complex but still precisely definable operation on DATs. The three requirements formulated informally above should be captured in terms of rules for DAT updates. The search for a suitable past chronoscope in which to incorporate the information contained in the flashback is guided, if not completely determined, by the structure of the DAT. When the interpreter backs up in the current chronoscope, using the existing filler rule, each node dominating the current node is common to a number of different past chronoscopes. A depth + rightmost-chronoscope-first search strategy should determine the "antecedent" for the flashback information. A suitable antecedent node carries the label whose descriptive information matches that of the clause that introduces the flashback, or satisfies the presuppositions of the first clause, if there is no overt trigger. For instance, *as she was calling the number* in (5.5c) has the node labeled

$$\langle\!\langle call,\, x,\, y_{\langle\!\langle number,\, y,\, +\rangle\!\rangle},\, +\rangle\!\rangle$$

as antecedent, representing the information contained in the first clause of (5.5a). Once this antecedent node has been found, it should be unplugged so that the new information can be incorporated.[6] There may be other linguistic constraints improving the efficiency of the search for an appropriate antecedent of a flashback. Such issues need more detailed consideration than can be given here, together with an extended empirical study of the variety of linguistic forms that induce flashbacks.

Suppose that a suitable antecedent has been found in a past chronoscope. The flashback procedure is then formalized as consisting of the following steps. Let C be the current chronoscope and c its current node; suppose furthermore that $a \in C$ is the lowest common ancestor of c and the plug p carrying the label matching the descriptive information of the first clause in the flashback.

(5.6)   Define **FB**(C)—the *flashback* on C—as follows:

i.   Retract C to C_a, dropping all nodes n dominated by a.

$$C_a = C - \{n \in C | a \text{ dominates } n\}$$

ii.   Expand C_a to C_p, adding all nodes n in the chronoscope $a \ll p$ of the DAT, n dominated by a and dominating p.

$$C_p = C_a \cup \{n \in N | a \text{ dominates } n \text{ and } n \text{ dominates } p\}$$

iii.   Unplug p by converting it to a hole, separating its start and its finish, and introducing a plug s labeled $start(T)$ as dependent node, where T is the type labeling p.

iv.   Set s to be the current node.

In terms of arrow kinematics, plugs have $\uparrow$ as left arrow. Unplugging p means that this $\uparrow$ is reversed to $\downarrow$ in C_p. This allows s, its starting point, to be introduced as a dependent node without violating the basic DAT rules, making it the new current node. Plugs are self-dual, like proper names in the NP category, and refer to objects that are considered within the perspective to lack internal structure. Unplugging a plug maps it into a full-fledged aspectual cube of oppositions, separating its start from its finish, which could not be distinguished before. When the interpretation proceeds, the new information contained in the flashback is represented by configurational DAT structure dependent upon p. It is important that none of the other nodes dependent upon p in D are accessible at this point, since the information in the flashback does not determine how it is temporally related to these old nodes. In the case of (5.5) the nodes representing Jane's wallet dropping, her hanging up, and her leaving the phone booth all disappear temporarily in the flashback, when the current chronoscope is redirected to the terminal node p. The information contained in the flashback is represented according to the regular DAT rules. When the interpretation backs up to a node dominating the current one, it must at some point back up to p itself. If p is plugged up again, the flashback is terminated. Plugging up a hole maps its start and finish to the plug, hiding its internal structure, as if the aspectual cube representing the space for its internal structure collapses to a self-dual event. In terms of arrows, this means that the left $\downarrow$ is reversed to $\uparrow$. After p is plugged again, the current chronoscope jumps back to C and revives c as current node. To encode this properly, C_p should be retracted to C_a and then expanded to C again, reversing the flashback operation to restore the original situation it departed from and letting the old nodes, introduced before the flashback as dependent upon p, reappear. We have seen in (5.5) that ending flashbacks is not always signaled by overt linguistic means. It would be a very interesting enterprise to determine what linguistic means do indicate the end of a flashback and how such information is otherwise inferred from the given information.

One apparently well-supported conjecture, based on DAT representations, requires that antecedents of flashbacks must be plugs, though they need not be terminal nodes. Furthermore, the label of such nodes must match the descriptive information of the clause triggering the flashback or satisfy its presuppositions. Illustrating with the example shown in (5.7), Caenepeel and Sandström (1992) argue that past perfect clauses that contain new descriptive information cannot trigger flashbacks.

(5.7)   ?He took two dirty glasses from the table and filled them
         with brandy. He had rinsed them out, and the glasses
         glittered in the sunlight.

Since it is neither presupposed nor entailed that he rinsed the glasses out before he filled them with brandy, the perfect second sentence gives new information that describes a causally disconnected event of rinsing, presumably occurring between the two events described by the first clause. Caenepeel and Sandström formulate a monotonicity constraint on episodic structures, requiring that in narratives a new event can be represented only by adding it to the open right end (the current node), and that it cannot be inserted between two events already represented as adjacent. Our discussion of flashbacks confirms this global constraint. Flashbacks may only be triggered by perfect clauses that copy the descriptive information of the antecedent, as in (5.5d) and (5.5e), or by presuppositions of such perfect clauses, as in (5.5g), accompanied with new information about Jane's calling. The effect of the monotonicity constraint can be observed in (5.8), where the first four sentences repeat the original (5.5a) and the last sentence is a new continuation.

(5.8)   Jane called the number. Her wallet fell on the floor.
         There was no answer, so she hung up. She left the phone
         booth.
         ?She had put a quarter on the phone book, but she needed
         more money.

In interpreting (5.8) in a DAT, the perfect clause *She had put a quarter on the phone book* would be represented by a sticker on the current node representing her leaving the phone booth. As all perfect clauses do, it entails the event that caused the state described by the perfect. This event should be located somewhere before her leaving the phone booth, but no specific information is given to determine how it is related to the other events described as having taken place before she left the phone booth. Hence, the interpretation of the subsequent simple past clause *she needed more money* lacks the directive aspectual information that controls where its node is to be located in the DAT, other than introducing it as a sister to the *leave* node. The definition of flashbacks (5.6) captured (1) that a flashback needs either matching or presupposition-linked labels in its antecedent, and (2) that the old information dependent upon the antecedent is temporarily disregarded during the incorporation of the new information contained in the flashback.

Perspectival refinement is a very general operation for unplugging plugs, if we allow *FB* to apply to a current node. This resolves the indeterminacy in the interpretation of filters, presented earlier. Filters offered an interpreter the choice of representing the information as a label on a hole or on a plug. This can now be redefined to require that all filters, representing accomplishments, are initially represented as plugs. If perspectival refinement is allowed to apply to the current node, in case it is a plug, the hole option for filters is just a special case of unplugging the current node. The refinement must however be triggered by the subsequent information, or its entailments and presuppositions. This reformulation makes the system of interpretation rules in DATs an effective, deterministic algorithm.

5.3 Perspectival Binding

Does all the information contained in the chronoscope remain accessible after plugging up the node to create a perspectival shift? Plugging up a hole seems to constrain indefinite antecedents for NP anaphora in an interesting and general way. Let us first look at (5.9) and (5.10) to see what happens with a simple example, varying the simple past and perfect systematically.

(5.9) Jane called [a number]$_i$. There was no answer, so she hung up. She left the phone booth.
   a. She noticed it$_i$ was missing the new initial digit 6.
   b. She noticed the number$_i$ was missing the new initial digit 6.
   c. She noticed it$_i$ in the paper.
   d. She had noticed it$_i$ in the paper.

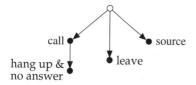

Figure 5.3
DAT for (5.9)

(5.10)   Jane had called [a number]ᵢ. There was no answer, so she
         had hung up. She had left the phone booth.
         a.   She noticed itᵢ was missing the new initial digit 6.
         b.   She had noticed itᵢ was missing the new initial digit 6.

The DAT for (5.9) is given in figure 5.3 with abbreviated labels. The *call*
node is labeled with a type containing a free parameter for the number. The
variations in (5.9a–d) test for linguistic constructions that may block unifi-
cation of this parameter with subsequent parameters representing the pronoun in the *notice* clause in texts without temporal adverbs. Assuming the
DAT rules, in (5.9a) the parameter for the pronoun occurs in a label of a
new node, right sister of the *leave* node. Since the descriptive information
about digits (which common sense tells us phone numbers are composed
of) helps us in this case, we interpret the pronoun fairly easily as corefer-
ring with *number*. If no clues could be taken from the new descriptive
information, it would be harder to interpret the pronoun as referring to the
number, as in (5.9c). Note that the chronoscope with the *leave* node inter-
venes between the current one and the one containing the antecedent. In
comparison to (5.9a), however, the explicit reintroduction of the number by
definite description in (5.9b) works to express coreference, even when the
descriptive information is included in a new chronoscope. When the parameter is embedded in a perfect sticker, as in (5.9d), attached to the *leave* node,
the coreferential interpretation is quite easy and acceptable, even without
help from the new descriptive information. Similarly, when the antecedent
is given in a perfect clause and the remaining clauses are all perfect, they
are all appended to the node introduced for Jane's noticing. Now the
antecedent and the pronoun are contained in the same chronoscope and the
coreference is easy. Apparently, the syntactic configurational distance in a
DAT between the node representing the information expressed using the
pronoun and the node labeled with its antecedent is a factor in binding
conditions for simple past clauses where the aspectual information plays
such an important role. Pronouns in descriptions of states are contained in
stickers, which may of course be imported into the chronoscope containing

their antecedent. The following general conjecture seems to capture these observations in terms of DAT structure:

> (5.11)   *Conjectured constraint on NP anaphora*
>
> 1.   A parameter in a parametric type representing an indefinite NP antecedent is accessible for unification with parameters in the labels of its dependent nodes or c-commanded right-sister nodes.
> 2.   After a node that dominates a node n with a free parametric type is plugged, it can be unified only with parameters representing pronouns in stickers portable to the chronoscope containing n.

The general question of which contexts prohibit something referred to previously by an indefinite NP from being referred to again by using a mere pronoun, instead requiring it to be "reintroduced" with descriptive labels to express coreference, must remain for future investigation. This book focuses primarily on the representation of intersentential temporal anaphora in DATs. From the discussion it is evident, however, that not only does the dynamic representation in DATs constrain temporal anaphora, but its chronoscopes apparently interact with the binding conditions on NP anaphora as well.

5.4   Scenes and Scenarios

We have assumed that a DAT contains a unique source node as the terminal node on its rightmost branch. But more sophisticated narrative texts may often lead to restructuring DATs to allow for multiple sources, issuing information that may be mutually partially incompatible. Dialogues are just one example requiring an explicit representation of multiple sources. But texts may be more subtle in introducing their protagonists as sources that must be inferred to be different from the main source, exploiting information given by the use of tense and aspect, compatibility of types, and the coherence constraint, as discussed in section 5.1. Such interesting issues lead quickly into the domain of literary theory, far beyond the intentions of this book. But it is possible to outline informally how DAT representations could be generalized to allow for information issued from more than one source.

In (5.5f) an example was given of a text that allowed us to interpret a simple past clause (in this case *Someone got hurt badly*) as representing the content of the protagonist's (in this case Jane's) thought or conclusions, instead of the descriptive information the source issues, which otherwise is warranting its claim to truth. The shift to the simple past to describe an earlier event after the two perfect clauses, represented as stickers on a node outside the chronoscope containing Jane's call, indicates that another source must be held responsible for this information. The speaker, issuing the information, is clearly distancing herself from the information Jane obtained from hearing the scream. To accommodate the requirements of this text, DATs may be enriched with a third dimension in which independent structures of nodes can be represented, labeled with information that must have been issued by other sources. The unique root must however still dominate all these nodes in the different sub-DATs, representing information from the different sources. This common root guarantees that the coherence constraint is satisfied, preserving a common background; it is the node to which stickers, representing common ground, may be imported, if their portability conditions allow it. As a fairly reliable test for when information should be represented as issuing from a different source, we can try to continue the text with incompatible nonsticker information. In the case of the story in (5.5f) we may receive the new information presented in (5.12).

(5.12)   When she ran there to help, she saw a junkie running around.

The information in (5.12) is incompatible with the information that the scream was caused by someone hurting someone else. That reinforces the representation of that information as issuing from a different source, presumably Jane, the caller, as the protagonist of the story, described by earlier clauses in the text.

If we allow for multiple sources in a three-dimensional DAT, we must still ensure that the different sub-DATs, each with its own source, converge via their embeddings in event structures. Though they describe the episode differently and each determines a different perspective on it, their embeddings must assign the same values in the event structure (modulo their source). When these conditions are fulfilled, a three-dimensional DAT is said to describe a *scenario*. Any part of an event structure that is described by a three-dimensional DAT is called a scenario, representing not only the narrator's information but also the subjective information of the protagonists. Each slice of this three-dimensional DAT with its unique source still describes an episode, but the different episodes may be classified as simultaneous, by mapping them onto a linear time line. Each such simultaneity class in described episodes constitutes a *scene*. A set of different scenes that share common background information, at the root of the three-dimensional DAT, together constitute a scenario. To suggest where this observation may lead, DAT rules may ultimately be formulated that apply to all nodes across scenes to incorporate new "public" information, if it is not introduced as a sticker on the root or other shared node dominating all scenes in the scenario. But such speculations on further developments lead us far beyond the more modest goals of this book.

Chapter 6
A Fragment of English

A fragment constitutes a laboratory environment for a theory of interpretation and should result in a formalization of the inferences and reasoning patterns intuitively judged to be acceptable. In working out a fragment, no claim is made that the methods apply only to that limited set of sentences. The fragment illustrates in all requisite details how the interpretation is designed and applied to a systematically generated set of sentences. A fragment requires a comprehensive set of rules, perspicuity of the syntax/ semantic interface, and a specification of the inference rules admitted. This makes the advantages of the system visible—but also its disadvantages, gaps, inadequacies, or idiosyncrasies.

This chapter describes a limited fragment of English that illustrates the core ideas of the dynamic interpretation of tense and aspect, using DATs and their chronoscopes as tools for semantic representation. It is intended as a starting point for developing a computational implementation, and it pulls together the various rules and principles of DAT interpretation in a systematic set of syntactic and representational rules for English. Section 6.1 gives the syntactic rules used to generate sentences, based on some elementary principles of generative syntactic theory. For some computational applications, it may be advantageous to recast such a generative syntax as a categorial syntax without movement rules, based on the principles of Lambek grammar. This possibility is briefly explored, and some issues are outlined for further research in this direction.[1] After the lexicon is presented, which encodes the aspectual properties of the descriptive vocabulary, the composition of aspect is specified in terms of arrow kinematics, originally encountered in chapter 2. Section 6.2 first presents the mapping of syntactic structure to the constituency of types and then recapitulates the DAT rules from chapter 3 and the portability constraints associated with stickers from chapter 4, tying them in with the syntax. Section 6.3 again presents the semantics of DATs in terms of embeddings in event structures constrained by the domain-specific reasoning rules from (3.8). Given the semantic constraints on temporal reasoning, the inferences admitted in the system illustrate once again the important differences between situated and logical entailments. A simple binary code of the relevant inflectional properties is outlined to capture other forms of temporal reasoning in terms of digital label transformations on DAT nodes. Finally, section 6.4 takes up some remaining logical and linguistic issues and unresolved puzzles.

6.1 Syntax and Lexicon

The grammar specified in this section generates some (but by no means all) examples discussed and analyzed in the previous chapters. Nevertheless, it provides a good basis for enriching this lexicon to allow for more sophisticated fragments. I choose to format the syntactic rules as consisting of a simple context-free phrase structure base, with a restricted set of rules to move certain constituents to other configurational positions. Issues such as thematic role assignment and argument structure are formulated easily within such a generative configurational structure. However, I also sketch a Lambek system without movement rules, intending thereby to emphasize the central structural properties these supposedly competing grammatical frameworks have in common, over the theoretical issues that divide them. It should be considered an advantage of the DAT representation system that it has not been welded onto any specific grammatical theory. To understand the principles at work in interpreting natural language, it is important to model the semantic processes first at a sufficiently abstract level, in order not to have to resolve all implementation-specific problems and idiosyncrasies inherent to one particular syntactic system. This is not to lessen the ultimate importance of such implementations, but only to indicate that the system, as it is presented here, still stands in need of further development of its syntactic component.

The well-formed sentences of the fragment are generated by the following rules; optional categories are indicated with brackets.

(6.1)   *Generative syntactic rules*
1.   CP → Comp IP
2.   IP → Spec VP_1 (ADJ)
3. VP_1 → Infl VP_2
4. VP_2 → DP VP_3
5. VP_3 → VP_4 (DP)
6. VP_4 → V_{asp} V/V
7.   DP → (Det) NP
8.   NP → (Adj) N/PN
9.   Infl → Pol (Tense) (Aspect) Agr
10. ADJ → Adv IP/PP
11. PP → Prep DP
12. Pol → 1/0

13. Tense → Past: $+/-$
14. Aspect → Perfect: $+/-$
15. Agr → Person: 1/2/3, Number: sing $+/-$, (Gender: fem $+/-$)

Adverbial phrases (Adv) are syntactically adjuncts to VP, so they are not part of the argument structure of the projections of V.[2] Semantically they describe properties or relations of events, so they cannot be constituents of events themselves, even though they affect the aspectual class of the IP. The specifier of IP position (Spec IP) is a landing site for VP-internal subjects, but it can also contain base-generated subjects of generic VPs in a proper-kind-predication context (see chapter 4).

Morphosyntactic principles, not fully specified here, arrange for the surface realization of the agreement features in Person: 1/2/3, Number: sing $+/-$, Past: $+/-$, and Perfect: $+/-$.[3] Perfect $-$ is expressed, for instance in English, by the progressive inflection *-ing* on the verbal head and insertion of the auxiliary verb *be* to carry the tense inflection. Owing to the lexically encoded static nature of the auxiliary verbs *be* and *have*, the resulting IP is interpreted as describing states—that is, represented in DATs as a portable *PROG* or *PERF* sticker. When the tense feature Past is not expressed, the V is infinitival, not finite. When the aspect feature Perfect is not expressed, the V is simply past or present. The combination of tense, aspectual, and Agr features, here applied to *walk*, is illustrated in (6.2).

(6.2) *Inflectional morphology*

Past $+$	Perfect $+$	3 sing	*walk*	$\Rightarrow$	*had walked*
Past $-$	Perfect $+$	2 pl	*walk*	$\Rightarrow$	*have walked*
Past $+$	Perfect $-$	3 pl	*walk*	$\Rightarrow$	*were walking*
Past $-$	Perfect $-$	1 sing	*walk*	$\Rightarrow$	*am walking*

The present tense (Past $-$) has been mostly disregarded, since it would introduce new issues concerning the relation between the source and described event not discussed in earlier chapters. It would require further analysis of the interaction between tense and generic information, beyond what was said in chapter 4. We discussed briefly in chapter 5 that including present tense would require an uprooting rule in DATs that requires more than this fragment is designed to handle.

Besides the generative syntactic rules, there is one rule to move DPs to Spec IP and one to raise verbal heads to Spec Infl, specified in (6.3).

(6.3) *Movement rules*
1. DP-movement
    $[_{\text{CP}} X \text{ DP } Y] \Rightarrow [_{\text{IP}} \text{DP}_i [X \text{ } PRO_i \text{ } Y]]$
2. V-movement
    $[_{\text{VP2}} X \text{ V } Y] \Rightarrow [_{\text{Infl}} V_i [X \text{ } e_i \text{ } Y]]$

Determiner Phrases (DPs) are base-generated in Spec IP, only if the VP is of the appropriate stative kind.[4] Semantically, the VP provides generic information represented as the nuclear scope of a sticker, relating to the subject DP by *GEN*. All the material outside the VP_1 is included in the restrictor of *GEN*, including as background all the stickers labeling the nodes dominating the current one in the entire chronoscope, and the other event-types embedded under *PROG*.[5] As we have seen, such *GEN* stickers have rather unrestricted portability conditions, capturing their "individual-level" predication. If the VP describes a simple transient state, the subject NP is generated inside the VP_1, but may be moved to Spec IP, again connecting to the VP by *GEN*. If it is not so moved, but remains in the VP, it is interpreted existentially through the embedding of the corresponding node labeled with a parametric type, representing the VP.

In English, auxiliary verbs, which include the aspectual verbs, raise only to receive inflection; that is, verb raising adjoins the verb to the affixes in Infl.

(6.4)   *Lexicon*
PROPER NAMES (PN) = {*Jane, John, noon*}
COMMON NOUNS (NP) = {*car*($x \uparrow$), *fence*($x \uparrow$), *police*($x \uparrow$), *phone booth*($x \uparrow$), *watch*($x \uparrow$), *hand*($x \uparrow$), *message*($x \uparrow$), *bomb*($x \uparrow$), *station*($x \uparrow$), *wallet*($x \uparrow$), *note*($x \uparrow$), *money*($x \downarrow$), *water*($x \downarrow$)}
ADJECTIVES (Adj) = {*happy*(x), *ill*(x)}
DETERMINERS (Det) = {*a*($T \uparrow$, $T' \uparrow$), *some*($T \uparrow$, $T' \uparrow$), *several*($T \uparrow$, $T' \uparrow$), *the*($T \uparrow$, $T' \uparrow$), *this*($T \uparrow$, $T' \uparrow$), *every*($T \downarrow$, $T' \uparrow$), *all*($T \downarrow$, $T' \uparrow$), *no*($T \downarrow$, $T' \downarrow$)}
VERBS (V)
V_1 = {*dial*($e \downarrow$, x), *sit*($e \downarrow$, x), *sigh*($e \downarrow$, x), *dance*($e \downarrow$, x), *lecture*($e \downarrow$, x), *leave*($e \uparrow$, x), *explode*($e \uparrow$, x), *arrive*($e \uparrow$, x), *jump*($e \uparrow$, x)}
V_2 = {*kill* ($e \uparrow$, x, y), *decipher*($e \uparrow$, x, y), *detect*($e \uparrow$, x, y), *find*($e \uparrow$, x, y), *read*($e \downarrow$, x, y), *write*($e \downarrow$, x, y), *drive*($e \downarrow$, x, y), *sing*($e \downarrow$, x, y), *clap*($e \downarrow$, x, y), *attempt*($e \downarrow$, x, y)}
V_{asp} = {*begin*($e \uparrow$, $T \uparrow$), *start*($e \uparrow$, $T \uparrow$), *resume*($e \uparrow$, $T \uparrow$), *keep*($e \downarrow$, $T \uparrow$), *continue*($e \downarrow$, $T \uparrow$), *stop*($e \uparrow$, $T \downarrow$), *complete*($e \uparrow$, $T \downarrow$), *finish*($e \uparrow$, $T \downarrow$), *end*($e \downarrow$, $T \downarrow$), *terminate*($e \downarrow$, $T \downarrow$), *cease*($e \downarrow$, $T \downarrow$), *halt*($e \downarrow$, $T \downarrow$)}
V_{aux} = {*be*(x, T), *have*(x, T)}
V_{att} = {*feel*(x, T), *think*(x, T)}
PREPOSITIONS (Prep) = {*along*($T \downarrow$), *through*($T \downarrow$), *for*($T \downarrow$), *in*($T \uparrow$)}
ADVERBS (Adv) = {*between*(T, T'), *after*(T, T'), *before*(T, T'), *since*($T \downarrow$, T'), *until*($T \uparrow$, T'), *when*(T, T'), *whenever*($T \downarrow$, T'), *while*(T, T')}

All lexical verbs that have dynamic aspectual force are lexically encoded by a left-up arrow on their event parameter, an external argument to the verbal head, corresponding to their representation as plugs in DATs. The static aspectual force of the verbs describing activities, represented as holes, is lexically encoded by the left-down arrow in their event parameter. When a type is introduced into the DAT and attached as a label to a new node, its event parameter is resolved by the introduction of a new node, connecting the type as a label to a plug, if $\uparrow$, and to a hole, if $\downarrow$. Types, lexically classified as descriptions of states, to be represented by stickers in the DATs, do not contain an event parameter. State-types do not have any intrinsic connection to the nodes they are appended to, since nodes are never introduced by stickers. When types are composed, the composition up to VP_2 inherits the down arrow, if any input type carries one. But when the DP in internal argument position of VP_4 is a measure term, or a count term ($\uparrow\uparrow$ or $\downarrow\uparrow$) that is assigned the thematic role of (completely) affected object, VP_3 is $\uparrow$. Of course, the subject DP may reverse this again in the composition of VP_2, if it is an indefinite mass term or bare plural. Prepositional phrases in ADJ may again reverse the arrow of the VP_1, unless the internal DP was a measure term. In (6.5) the composition of arrows is illustrated with some simple examples.

(6.5) *Composition of aspect*
    a.   Jane moved furniture for an hour.
        $(\uparrow + (\downarrow + \downarrow)) + \downarrow = \downarrow$
    b.   Jane pushed her bike.
        $\uparrow + (\downarrow + \uparrow) = \downarrow$ (*bike* is instrument)
    c.   Jane sold her bike.
        $\uparrow + (\uparrow + \uparrow) = \uparrow$
    d.   Jane strolled through the dark alleys.
        $(\uparrow + \downarrow) + \downarrow = \downarrow$
    e.   Jane walked a mile through the dark alleys.
        $(\uparrow + ((\downarrow + \uparrow) + \downarrow)) = \uparrow$
    f.   Jane read.
        $\uparrow + \downarrow = \downarrow$
    g.   Jane read the note.
        $\uparrow + (\downarrow + \uparrow) = \uparrow$ (*note* is affected object)
    h.   Jane read the note in a moment.
        $(\uparrow + (\downarrow + \uparrow)) + \uparrow = \uparrow$
    i.   Jane read the note for a while.
        $(\uparrow + (\downarrow + \uparrow)) + \downarrow = \downarrow$

The principles for the composition of aspect constitute a calculus using only syntactic information, since the lexically encoded arrows, the thematic roles, and the configurational structure determine how composition affects the arrows. This constitutes a syntactic encoding of the aspectual control information at the type level. When the type is used to label a node in a DAT, this encoding is used to determine the nature of the new node and its label expanding the DAT (see section 6.2).

Categorial grammars eliminate the phrase structure component by projecting information that is encoded in its rules into the structured types.[6] We assume the categories S, N, DP, Adj, PP and assign them the following types, based on the primitives e for entities and t for truth-values:

(6.6)   *Type assignment*
type (S) = t, type (DP) = $((e, t), t)$,
type (N) = type (Adj) = type (PP) = (e, t)

This notation means that the type (a, b) is the type of functions from a-type objects to b-type objects, where a and b are variables for types. There are three type-forming connectives ($\bullet$, /, and \) in a Lambek categorial grammar, creating composition $X \bullet Y$ and the functor categories $A/B = B\backslash A = $ (type (B), type (A)). The categorial types are interpreted as sets of expressions, subsets of **S** obtained by closing the set of lexical items under concatenation.

(6.7)   *Complex types formation*
$A \bullet B = \{xy \in \mathbf{S} | x \in A \ \& \ y \in B\}$ [def. $\bullet$]
$C/B = \{x \in \mathbf{S} | \forall y \in B, xy \in C\}$ [def. /]
$A\backslash C = \{y \in \mathbf{S} | \forall x \in A, xy \in C\}$ [def. \]

To compute the complex types, correlated with their intended semantics, the following reduction laws are used in Lambek systems:

(6.8)   *Lambek reduction laws*
   1. Application
      $X/Y : f \quad Y : a \Rightarrow X : f(a)$
      $Y : a \quad Y\backslash X : f \Rightarrow X : f(a)$
   2. Composition
      $X/Y : f \quad Y/Z : g \Rightarrow X/Z : \lambda v \, f(g\,(v))$
      $Z\backslash Y : g \quad Y\backslash X : f \Rightarrow Z\backslash X : \lambda v \, f(g\,(v))$
   3. Associativity (optional)
      $(Z\backslash X)/Y : f \Leftrightarrow Z\backslash(X/Y) : \lambda v_1 \, \lambda v_2 \, f(v_2)(v_1)$
   4. Lifting
      $X : a \Rightarrow Y/(X\backslash Y) : \lambda v \, v \,(a)$
      $X : a \Rightarrow (Y/X)\backslash Y : \lambda v \, v \,(a)$
   5. Division
      $X/Y : f \Rightarrow (X/Z)/(Y/Z) : \lambda v_1 \, \lambda v_2 \, f(v_1 \,(v_2))$
      $Y\backslash X : f \Rightarrow (Z\backslash Y)/(Z\backslash X) : \lambda v_1 \, \lambda v_2 \, f(v_1 \,(v_2))$

These rules may not constitute the leanest set of reduction laws, but for applications they are very convenient and explicit. It is known, for instance, that the combination of Division with Application yields Composition.

To specify the Lambek grammar for a fragment more or less (weakly) equivalent to the generative grammar specified in (6.1)–(6.4), the remaining categories are defined from the assumed ones.

(6.8)   *Defined types*
Det = DP/N
V = (DP\S)/DP
Adv = S\S
Adj = N/N

The definition of Infl in Lambek systems is less straightforward. If we define Infl = S/S, and it is to apply to the verbal head, its type must be shifted. The requisite type is, for transitive verbs at least, (DP\S)/DP/((DP\S)/DP), which takes a transitive verb (VP_4) with an object DP slot and a subject DP slot into the same, but now inflected, verbal head. But there is no legitimate, semantically warranted type-shifting operation from S/S to (DP\S)/DP/((DP\S)/DP), given the free semigroup semantics of the functor connectives in this directionally mixed form of composition. To resolve this problem and preserve the intended semantics, we need to make the composition of types sensitive to the head of a composition, giving up the symmetry of • and replacing it with two head-sensitive operations. Associativity is also abandoned as a reduction law. The trees must be marked for the head of the composition throughout, so that the lexical head may be retrieved by tracing the continuous path of heads to the terminal node. If this head-sensitivity is implemented, the extraction of the verbal head to Infl may be obtained by defining an extraction operation A   B to extract a verbal head A from a type B, with the intended semantics defined in (6.9).

(6.9)   *Extraction in a Lambek grammar*
$[\![A \Uparrow B]\!] = \{y | \forall x \forall z [(z = x \otimes y \ \& \ x \in [\![A]\!]) \Rightarrow z \in [\![B]\!]]\}$
where $x \otimes y$ is a binary wrapping operation on headed trees such that inflected auxiliary verbs *be* or *have* are inserted before the verbal head, if any, and other inflection features affect the verbal head itself.

To consider the consequences of defining extraction in such a headed Lambek grammar would lead us too far from the intentions of this chapter. The details require far more than a short detour into the technicalities of the algebraic semantics of Lambek grammars and their Gentzen presentation. The point illustrated by this discussion is merely that for computational applications it may be considered preferable to recast the generative syntax in a categorial system with a clear semantic interpretation. There seem no principled obstacles to doing so, if head-sensitive composition is admitted as a reduction law in Lambek grammars.

6.2 DAT Rules

Before we turn to the construction of DATs by the interpretation of texts, the mapping from the syntactic structure of clauses to their types, representing their descriptive content, should be specified. To compose the type, each syntactic rule is associated with a semantic one. Lexical material is represented as relations with appropriate argument structure, and composition is essentially function composition of roles. With a slight but familiar abuse of notation, the category label is used in the type to stand for the type corresponding to an expression of that category.

(6.10)   *Semantic representation rules*

1. CP → Comp IP
    Representation
    Comp IP $\approx>$ Comp (c, IP)

    c is the current node where IP is introduced into the DAT

2. IP → Spec VP_1 (ADJ)
    Type representation
    Spec VP_1 (ADJ) $\approx>$ ADJ$([y|\text{Spec}[x|\text{VP}_1(x, y)]])$

3. VP_1 → Infl VP_2
    Type representation
    Infl VP_2 $\approx>$ $T = T$

4. VP_2 → DP VP_3
    Type representation
    DP VP_3 $\approx>$ $[T|\text{DP}]\,([x|\text{VP}_3])$

5. VP_3 → VP_4 (DP)
    Type representation
    VP_4 (DP) $\approx>$ $[T', T|\text{DP}]\,([x|\text{VP}_4])$

6. VP_4 → V_{asp} V/V
    Type representation
    V_{asp} V $\approx>$ $[x|\text{V}_{\text{asp}}\,(x, [x|\text{V}\,(e, x)])]$
    V $\approx>$ $[x, y|\text{V}\,(e, x, y)]$

7. DP → (Det) NP
    Type representation
    (Det) NP $\approx>$ $[T', T|\text{Det}\,(T, T')]\,[x|\text{NP}\,(x)]$

8. NP → (Adj) N
    Type representation
    (Adj) N $\approx>$ $[x|\text{Adj}\,(x)\ \&\ \text{N}\,(x)]$

9. Infl → Pol (Tense) (Aspect) Agr
    Type representation
    Pol (Tense) (Aspect) Agr $\approx>$ T

Below, the Infl features are represented as digital bit-strings on which computations are defined that capture valid inferences. In the type representation the features are not further specified.

10. ADJ → Adv IP/PP
     Type representation
     Adv IP $\approx>$ Adv (T)
     PP $\approx>$ $[e|PP\ (e)]$

11. PP → Prep DP
     Type representation
     Prep DP $\approx>$ $[e|Prep\ (DP,\ e)]$

12. Pol → 1/0
     Type representation
     $1 \approx> [T|«T,\ +»]$
     $0 \approx> [T|«T,\ -»]$

13. Tense → Past: $+/-$
     Representation
     PAST $+\ \approx> [e|e < e'|= «\textbf{source},\ x,\ +»]$
     PAST $-\ \approx> [e|e \supseteq e'|= «\textbf{source},\ x,\ +»]$

Tense is not represented within the label, since it affects the DAT, not the constituency of its labels.[7] Its contribution to the information is captured here as a constraint between nodes introduced with simple-past tense event descriptions and the source node.

14. Aspect → Perfect: $+/-$
     Type representation
     Perfect $+\ \approx> PERF«T»$
     Perfect $-\ \approx> PROG«T»$

15. Agr → Person: 1/2/3, Number: sing $+/-$, (Gender: fem $+/-$)
     Type representation
     Person 1 $\approx> [y|y = x_{«\textbf{source},x,\ +»}]$
     Person 2 $\approx> [y|y = x_{«\textbf{source},x,\ -»}]$
     Person 3 $\approx> x$

The number and gender features can be encoded similarly as restrictions on the parameters they affect.

   The composition of types specifies how the labels are created for the nodes in a DAT. The rules for constructing DATs, collected in (6.11), determine the architecture of the representation and direct the flow of information. In (6.11) let T be the type composed from the inflected clause and c be the current node in the given DAT, and assume that the type is classified with respect to its aspectual class, based on the arrow composition associated with the types.

(6.11)   *Rules for DAT construction*
1. If T is a state-type, append T as a sticker to c, if c is a plug, and append T to the next node, if c is a hole.
2. If T is an activity-type, introduce a hole h, set $h = c$, and label h with T.
3. If T is an accomplishment-type or achievement-type, introduce a plug p, set $p = c$, and label p with T.
4. If the extension of the DAT resulting from applying rules 1–3 is inconsistent, then plug the closest dominating node necessary to remove the inconsistency, make it the current node, and reapply the rules.
5. If the current node of a DAT is a hole, the new node is introduced as a dependent node.
6. If the current node of a DAT is a plug, the new node is introduced as its right sister.
7. Perspectival refinement (a = lowest ancestor of p and c) **FB**(C)—the *flashback* on C:
   i.   Retract C to C_a.
         $C_a = C - \{n \in C | a \text{ dominates } n\}$
   ii.   Expand C_a to C_p.
         $C_p = C_a \cup \{n \in N | a \text{ dominates } n \text{ and } n$
                dominates $p\}$
   iii. Unplug p by converting it to a hole and introducing a plug s labeled *start*(T) as dependent node where T is the type labeling p.
   iv.   Set s to be the current node.

As for operations on DATs, the portability conditions on stickers need to be specified.

(6.12)   *Portability of stickers*
1. If a node n is labeled with a sticker, transmit the sticker freely to the labels of all nodes that n dominates.
2. If a node n is labeled with a sticker *PERF(T)*, transmit the sticker to all right sisters of n, and to all nodes dominated by nodes in the chronoscope containing the node labeled T, but preceded by it.

3. If a node n is labeled with a type T, then the sticker $PROG(T)$ on a dependent node may be transmitted upward to any node n dominates.
4. If a node n is labeled with a sticker $GEN(T, T')$, then the sticker can be imported to any node that is compatible with T.

These are all the rules required to represent the information obtained from the interpretation of a text in DATs. Together they constitute a mapping from the configurational syntax to the DAT representation.

6.3 Semantics

DATs are formal objects that need an interpretation in suitable models, before inference can be formally characterized as an information-preserving operation on DATs. DATs are intended to be interpreted in event structures, which are event frames with an assignment of event-types of the events that support them, satisfying the constraints on temporal reasoning discussed in chapter 3.

(6.13) *Definition of event frame*
An *event frame* consists of a set of events E ordered by temporal inclusion $\rightarrow$ ($x \rightarrow y - y$ is a temporal part of x) and temporal precedence $<$ ($x < y - x$ occurs before y), together with an assignment to each T in $TYPE$ of a set of events $[\![T]\!]$, the *extension* of T, such that the temporal inclusion is a partial order, temporal precedence is a strict partial order, and their interaction is constrained by
 • *monotonicity*: if $y \rightarrow x$ and $y < z$, then $x < z$
 • *convexity*: if $x < y < z$ and $u \rightarrow x$ and $u \rightarrow z$, then $u \rightarrow y$[8]

DATs are interpreted in such event frames by embeddings, mapping nodes to events preserving the temporal relations and satisfying certain additional conditions.

(6.14) *Definition of embedding*
A function f mapping a DAT into a model M *is an embedding* when
  i.   for every arrow $\pi_N (n) \rightarrow n$, $f(\pi_N(n)) \rightarrow f(n)$[9]
  ii. if n c-commands n', then $f(n) < f(n')$,
  iii. $f(n) \models T$, where T is the type labeling n.

(6.15) Let D be a DAT and f an embedding of it into an event structure. Then D *describes* f iff

for all nodes n in D and all types T
if T labels n in D, then $f(n) \models T$ in the event structure

The event structures that are suitable models for temporal reasoning must in addition satisfy at least the following constraints.

(6.16)   *Semantic constraints for temporal reasoning*

1. Maximality of event-types
   If $e \models T$ and e is part of e' and $e' \models T$, then $e = e'$.
2. Downward persistence for stickers
   If $e \models T$, is a sticker, and e' is part of e, then $e' \models T$.
3. If T is part of T', then
   $\forall e$ if $e \models PROG(T)$, then $e \models PROG(T')$.
4. $e \models PERF(T)$ iff $\exists e' < e, e' \models T$.
5. If $e \models T$ and e' is part of e, then $e' \models PROG(T)$.
6. If $e \models PROG(T))$ and T is classified as an ACTIVITY, then $e \models T$.
7. If $e < e'$, then $e < \text{start}(e')$.
8. $e \models \textbf{START}(T)$ iff $\exists e', e' \models T$ and $e = \text{start}(e')$.
9. $\forall e$ if $e \models PROG(T)$, then $e \models PERF(\textbf{START}(T))$.

In reasoning with DATs, the conclusion describes an event via the embedding into the event structure of the current node in a DAT representing the information obtained by processing its premises. The premises together describe the entire episode, ending with the event also described by the conclusion. This context-dependence of temporal reasoning is formalized in the notion of situated entailment in DATs.

(6.17)   *Situated entailment*

Let D be a DAT for the premises $T_1, \ldots, T_n$ and let c be its current node. Then $T_1, \ldots, T_n \models T$ iff for all event structures S and all embeddings f of D into S, if $T_1, \ldots, T_n$ describes $f(D)$, then $f(c)$ is of type T.

The situated entailments are preserved for all perfect sticker conclusions in DAT extensions, so for information about such perfect states the inference relation is monotonic, corresponding to their portability. No matter what information is added to the premises, if a perfect tense conclusion can be inferred at some point, the same conclusion can always be inferred at any later point in the interpretation. But, of course, the situated entailments of other information, represented by the other labels on the current node, are not monotonic, since a change of the current chronoscope in perspectival shift loses some of the situated entailments valid in the previous chronoscope. Ordinarily compatible stickers can be added to a given DAT for the premises without affecting the valid situated entailments. But adding new nodes to the DAT, incorporating additional dynamic information, is bound to affect the set of situated entailments derivable from it.

In designing further computational procedures, a digital code may be defined on which some very simple transformations can be specified to capture inferences based on Infl features and aspectual verbs. A brief outline of this encoding is given below.

(6.18)   *Binary encoding of Infl features*
         Person 1 = 100
         Person 2 = 010
         Person 3 = 001
         Singular + = 1
         Singular − = 0
         Other features in Tense and Aspect + = 1, − = 0

The aspectual verbs may be encoded in a digital representation of triples. The four aspectual verbs on the front of the aspectual cube in chapter 2 are encoded with 0 in the first bit, the other four on the back with 1 in the first bit. The second bit represents the on (1)/off (0) input state, and the third bit the on (1)/off (0) output after the transition described by the aspectual verb. All eight corners on the aspectual cube are digitally coded as in figure 6.1.

(6.19)   *Aspectual verbs encoded in binary triples*
         start, begin   = 001   stop   = 110
         finish   = 010   resume = 101
         continue   = 011   keep   = 111
         refrain/nonstart   = 000   end   = 100

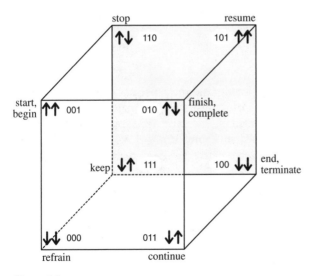

Figure 6.1
Digital code of aspectual verbs

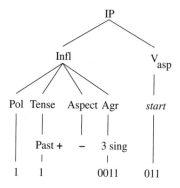

Figure 6.2
Digital code composition for *he started*

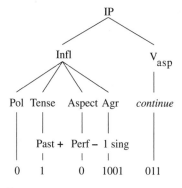

Figure 6.3
Digital code composition for *I was not continuing*

This digital code of Infl constituents and the aspectual verbs compiles into a complex code carrying all the constraint information controlling the descriptive information encoded in the type labeling the node. This is shown in (6.20) and illustrated in figures 6.2 and 6.3, corresponding to (6.20a) and (6.20c), respectively, where — is used if the feature is not defined.

(6.20) a. *he started*   11– 0011 001
        b. *you have resumed*   101 0101 101
        c. *I was not continuing*   010 1001 011
        d. *I had stopped*   111 1001 110

Now we see a simple relationship between the encoding of *I was not continuing* (6.20c) and *I had stopped* (6.20d). The outside first and third bits in the first triple are reversed 1/0, "negated" in a sense; the following quadruple coding the Agr features is preserved; and the first and third bits in the last triple are again reversed. If we assume that the presuppositions are also preserved, the equivalence between the two can be formalized as an operation on the encoding, reversing the first and third bits in both triples and pres_rving everything else.

(6.21)   *was not* V_{asp}-*ing* $\Leftrightarrow$ dual (*was not*) dual(V_{asp})-*ed* $\Leftrightarrow$ dual (010) dual (011) $\Leftrightarrow$ 111 110 $\Leftrightarrow$ *had* V_{asp}-*ed*

These encodings and inferences as transformations on them are new examples of situated inferences based on aspectual adverbs, even though they may be embedded in *PROG* and *PERF* stickers, as in the example above. The clauses could be read with an implicit "at that time," and only the local context is relevant in determining the reference of indefinites. It remains to be seen whether the encodings can be generalized for other auxiliary verbs and verbal heads. It is likely that aspectual adverbs like *no longer, still, not yet,* and *already* will have to come into play to constrain the local context and ensure preservation of the presuppositions.

To complete the semantics of DATs, the constraints on aspectual verbs from chapter 2 are repeated here as inference rules, allowing content-preserving substitution of labels in DATs.

(6.22)   *Constraints on aspectual verbs*
1. $\forall s$ [$s \models$ «*STOP*, «$R, x_1, \ldots, x_n,$ +», +» $\Leftrightarrow$
       $s \models$ «*START*, «$R, x_1, \ldots, x_n,$ −», +»]
2. $\forall s$ [$s \models$ «*FINISH*, «$R, x_1, \ldots, x_n,$ −», +» $\Leftrightarrow$
       [$s \models$ «*START*, «$R, x_1, \ldots, x_n,$ −», +»]]
3. $\forall s$ [$s \models$ «*STOP*, «$R, x_1, \ldots, x_n,$ +», +» $\Leftrightarrow$
       [$s \models$ «*RESUME*, «$R, x_1, \ldots, x_n,$ −», +»]]
4. $\forall s$ [$s \models$ «*END*, «$R, x_1, \ldots, x_n,$ +», +» $\Leftrightarrow$
       [$s \models$ «*KEEP*, «$R, x_1, \ldots, x_n,$ −», +»]]
5. $\forall s$ [$s \models$ «*END*, «$R, x_1, \ldots, x_n,$ +», +» $\Leftrightarrow$
       [$s \models$ «*CONTINUE*, «$R, x_1, \ldots, x_n,$ −», +»]]
6. $\forall s$ [$s \models$ «*STOP*, $T,$ +» $\Leftrightarrow s \models$ «*KEEP*, $T,$ −»]
7. $\forall s$ [$s \models$ «*FINISH*, $T,$ +» $\Leftrightarrow s \models$ «*CONTINUE*, $T,$ −»]
8. $\forall s$ [$s \models$ «*RESUME*, $T,$ +» $\Leftrightarrow s \models$ «*END*, $T,$ −»]
7. $\forall s$ [$s \models$ «*START*, $T,$ +» $\Leftrightarrow s \models$ «*NOT-START*, $T,$ −»]

These constraints on aspectual verbs create the oppositions defining the aspectual cube. The projection of presuppositions of aspectual verbs has not been analyzed in the dynamic DAT representations, but remains for future research.

6.4 Further Issues

The metaconstraints on DATs have been fully formalized in section 3.4. They are not repeated here. But it should be clear that in any DAT the source node is always required to be the terminal node of the rightmost chronoscope. It may be dominated by nodes representing what is going on at the source, for example, who is speaking or what time it is.

Since little has been made explicit in the syntax about the way verbal heads assign thematic roles to their arguments, a few remarks on this topic are in order. Tenny (1992) argues, within Jackendoff's (1990) framework of Lexical Conceptual Structures, that any account of thematic roles needs to be linked to aspectual roles associated with the argument structure of verbal heads. Although the system of DAT representation has no new insights to contribute on the principles governing thematic role assignment in generative syntax, the semantic realism of the philosophical theory underlying DAT representation may provide a good basis for clarifying the connection between constituents in event-types, the aspectual classes, and thematic roles. It has been argued above that for a proper classification of the event-types with respect to the aspectual classes, thematic roles are required in addition to the pure argument structure of the descriptive types. The characterization of thematic roles as restrictions on parameters in types can be defined as follows.

(6.23)   *Thematic role definitions*

source	$[x, T|\text{«CAUSE}, x, T, +\text{»}]$
instrument	$[x, T|\text{«CARRIER}, x, T, +\text{»}]$
goal	$[x, T|\text{«CHANGE}, T, x, +\text{»}]$
immediately affected	$[x, T|\text{«AFFECT}, T, x, +\text{»}]$
result	$[x, T|\text{«CAUSE}, T, x, +\text{»}]$
experiencer	$[x, T|\text{«V}_a x, T, +\text{»}]^{10}$

No claim is made here that these are the only thematic roles needed in a semantic theory, or that the relations **CAUSE, CARRIER, CHANGE, AFFECT** have any conceptual or cognitive priority over other relations. The definition is merely intended to show that thematic role assignment is easily captured in terms of restricted parameters on DAT labels.

It is a common assumption in generative syntax that the verbal head assigns thematic roles to the subject DP before it is moved to Spec IP. Aspectual and auxiliary verbs do not assign thematic roles, which can be understood as supporting their logical character as controllers of the descriptive information-flow. Perhaps logical constants could in general be characterized by the inability to assign thematic roles to their argument structure.

To conclude this chapter, a brief discussion of an "ancient" semantic puzzle may indicate what has been gained by this DAT account of dynamic interpretation of tense and aspect (though it also restores a certain modesty, by serving as a reminder that after more than two decades of flourishing research on quantification and reference, it still remains to be solved). The puzzle was first described by Gruber (1976) and accordingly is named here *Gruber's puzzle*.[11] The puzzle's original formulation is given in (6.24).

(6.24) *Gruber's puzzle*
    a.   Every oak grew out of an acorn.
    b.   An oak grew out of every acorn.
    c.   Every acorn grew into an oak.
    d.   *An acorn grew into every oak.

Why is (6.24d) unacceptable? Jackendoff (1983) offers a more general description of the phenomenon.

> If the indefinite NP precedes the quantifier, thematic relations come into play: when the quantified NP is source, quantification is acceptable, but when the quantified NP is goal, quantification is not possible. (p. 207)

If we paraphrase the clauses with *become* and *come from*, as in (6.25), it seems the pattern is entirely parallel.

(6.25) a.   Every oak came from an acorn.
    b.   An oak came from every acorn.
    c.   Every acorn became an oak.
    d.   An acorn became every oak.

In terms of dynamic semantics, the universal DPs are considered stative and preserve the context, whereas the existential ones are dynamic and context-changing. Clearly, *grow out of* requires a source argument in its object DP, but *grow into* requires a goal argument. We see now that quantified goal arguments are unacceptable when the verb describes change and the subject DP is existential. This must be related to another asymmetry, illustrated in (6.26).

(6.26) a.   Every present consisted of a book.
    b.   *A book became every present.

The stative relation *consist of* is perfectly fine in describing a relation between a universally quantified subject and an existential object DP, as in (6.26a). But if we want to describe the event that must have caused that state, it seems that an existential subject DP cannot be source of a dynamic relation with a universally quantified object DP as goal. Given the assumptions we made about the mapping of DP/VP structure to the restrictor and nuclear scope, we may formulate the following conjecture. If the restrictor contains the source argument, moved to Spec IP from a VP-internal position, the nuclear scope may contain the goal of the relation described, but not vice versa. Accordingly, quantified source arguments may be moved into Spec IP and be expressed as subjects, whereas quantified sources cannot be so moved, when they are base-generated as VP-internal arguments. Whatever the ultimate solution to this puzzle may be, it clearly must be couched in an account that explains the important semantic relations among dynamic and stative transitions, thematic roles, and quantification.

Chapter 7
Epilogue

Language is a big juggling act.
Jon Barwise and John Perry

This final chapter offers further reflection on the nature of the system of semantic representation developed in this book. Taking a somewhat more philosophical stance, it considers what the results of this kind of linguistic analysis contribute to cognitive science. This naturalized, causal theory of content requires clarification of the nature of parameters, if they are part of the world on a par with objects and constituents of events and situations. Ultimately, a full-fledged semantic theory should also account for misunderstandings, errors of interpretation, failures of inference, and other forms of breakdown in communication. The chapter closes with suggestions for developing the DAT representation system into such a broader and more generally applicable theory of interpretation and information.

7.1 Cognition and Semantic Representation

Parametric types play an important role in this account of the dynamic interpretation of tense and aspect in natural language. The linguistic expressions about what happened are represented in DATs, which integrate their descriptive, aspectual, and perspectival information. The embeddings of DATs into event structures provide the essential connections that determine what the information obtained in the process of interpretation is about, which situations are described, or which episode is referred to. On the one hand, it may seem that the DATs provide a syntactic, configurational, and hence formal means of representing information, because it is specified independently what forms DATs may take and rules of inference have been formulated in terms of DAT structure. Yet DATs do not constitute another linguistic level, mediating between the syntactic structure of the linguistic input and its intended models, like the translations of ordinary English into the language of intensional logic in Montague Grammar with indirect interpretation. Considering the DAT representations to be linguistic objects of a formal language would rest on a serious misconception of the entire enterprise of dynamic interpretation in this information-theoretic approach. Types consists of relations, objects that stand in such relations, and polarities. Parameters stand in relations to such entities and to other parameters as well. They are all constituents of the world represented as sequences. Parametric types serve to classify different events as similar in the partially described respects, as carriers of the same partial information and hence capable of playing the same causal role in the flow of information.

Specifying what possible forms a semantic representation may take is a prerequisite for defining how different representations can contain the same information, that is, be informationally equivalent and admit the same situated inferences. Without a solid characterization of the informational equivalence of representations we cannot even begin to model human reasoning. The fundamental semantic operation of substituting objects for parameters, grounding the information in the event structures, requires this independent characterization of informational equivalence. In the DAT representations situated inferences are defined by the embeddings: episodes that support the same DATs carry the same information (i.e., they are informationally indistinguishable). Any difference between one situation and another can only be detected if information represented in a DAT is supported by the one and not by the other. Situated inference is the core semantic concept of the dynamic interpretation in DATs, since it determines how information represented by interpreting linguistic input may later be retrieved and reported. Hence, the module or level at which these notions are defined is itself semantic in nature, relative to the system it serves to interpret, in the present case a fragment of English. Once a semantic process is well understood, it may be reflected in a syntactic code by a corresponding formal operation or symbolic transformation. This is just what is accomplished in the familiar logical systems, where inference is captured in terms of formal operations on strings of symbols in natural deduction systems, axiomatic proofs, or Gentzen sequents. But such operations must be guaranteed to simulate the corresponding semantic processes correctly by a completeness proof, showing that all and only all semantically valid transitions are captured in the admitted syntactic operations. In fact, any arbitrary number of intervening levels may be postulated between the natural-language syntax and the described domain, each with its own formal code and "daisy-chained" by some appropriate structure-preserving mapping. The real methodological question is whether such intervening levels produce any additional explanatory insights that could not already be obtained in directly modeling reasoning by dynamic interpretation in event structures. The DAT representations are in this sense syntactic reflections of semantic processes. The portability conditions on the stickers, for instance, are formulated in terms of the configurational structure of the DATs, that is, as inference rules within its proof theory. This book has not been intended to include a study of the logical properties of DAT representations. It remains to prove the completeness of an axiomatized theory of the DAT representations and their semantics in terms of embeddings into event structures satisfying the additional temporal constraints. But future research efforts may be directed toward demonstrating the logical properties of the system, guaranteeing that the temporal reasoning on DATs is indeed provably semantically correct. It is to be expected that the operations of unplugging and plugging up that affect the perspective introduce new complexity issues in proving the completeness, leading beyond merely recasting the system in the familiar form of a modal logic.[1]

The very distinction between the syntactic component of a system and its semantics is only a relative one between its levels or modules. One and the same component may interpret a "lower"-level system, while simultaneously serving as syntactic specification of another interpreter in a hierarchy of representational levels. General methodological and pragmatic considerations of formal efficiency, simplicity of operations, and explanatory adequacy then determine that preference is given to the account with fewer components or distinct representational levels. In DAT representations three kinds of information are encoded together, which may be thought of as belonging to different levels: (1) the open/closed properties of nodes encode the aspectual control of the information flow, (2) the arrows connecting nodes encode temporal part-whole relations between events that support the respective types labeling the nodes, and (3) the types themselves represent the descriptive information about the events or episode. Yet it remains quite straightforward to define the situated entailments as relations between DATs, despite this mixing of different kinds of information.[2]

Any dispute over the issue of whether the "real" status of DATs is syntactic or semantic is void. DATs do offer a configurational level at which temporal reasoning is captured in terms of formal operations, but they are not *about* the external world. Rather, they are part of it and hence play their causal role in architecturally structuring the flow of information.

7.2 Referring with Parameters

If parameters are on a par with objects and they are not expressions of a formal language, like the variables of predicate logic, there is a substantive philosophical question concerning their relation to objects the world consists of. Parameters are not part of our directly observable world in the same way that physical objects are or anything else that we can encounter

Figure 7.1
Drawing the altitude with an auxiliary construction

is. The world lends itself to an infinite variety of structuring relations, only a few of which are actually useful for our communicative purposes. Any part of the world, no matter how large or complex in structure, supports some parametric type in some DAT. The constituent structure of the type determines how the object supporting it is represented, related to other constituents of the representation, and traced in subsequent updates.

Dynamic interpretation uses parametric types in DATs in a way comparable to the way auxiliary constructions are used in geometrical demonstrations or proofs. This comparison is best elucidated with the familiar example of an auxiliary construction in geometry. As shown in figure 7.1, using the compass to draw two intersecting circles with identical diameter from each of the two angles on the base of an isosceles triangle, we efficiently determine the location of its altitude (the line from the top intersecting the base at a straight angle). This auxiliary construction, requiring a compass as instrument, is the only systematic procedure available to us to draw the desired line. If we had no recourse to it, we could only experiment at random, trying to locate the altitude correctly, drawing a line and measuring its angle with the base, continuing this possibly ad infinitum, without ever being assured of success. Parameters are just such auxiliary constructions of the dynamic interpretation of discourse or texts. They offer the necessary flexibility to classify what is happening into recurrent similarities. If a simple parametric type with a positive polarity is supported by a plug, a fundamental, atomic representation of part of the world has been obtained with stable identity and individuation conditions. Within the limits of the given perspective a plug offers maximal descriptive information about what is happening at that time, since it supports all the types in its chronoscope as stickers embedded under *PROG*. If a rigid designator (i.e., a name insensitive to context shifts) is at that time introduced for the plug, later clauses may use it in a causal chain to express temporal coreference or simultaneity no matter in what context. This, I suggest, is the semantic analogue of drawing the altitude in the auxiliary construction. Using parameters is like using the compass in constructing the representation of the information obtained by interpreting natural language. Parameters allow us to determine reference in context and then fix how we refer to it in a way that is desensitized to any subsequent context change. Hence, parameters as abstract, theoretical entities do not just come out of the blue; instead, they arise as by-products of our interpretations of linguistic descriptions. We use them in a given interpretation to model our reasoning about a particular described episode. We may modify or freeze the structure in which they occur, replace them, make them (in)accessible to other stages of the interpretation process, or identify them later with another parameter. They are the theoretical entities essential to the dynamic theory of meaning and content designed to model our temporal reasoning and the flow of information. Our use of such auxiliary constructions in geometry as well as in semantics is perfectly legitimate, as long as we also offer precise procedures for how the constructions are carried out, used, and manipulated in the representations. Their existence is entirely justified from the point of view of the working semanticist, if postulating such objects is required for a useful empirical theory of informative content, situated inference, and reasoning.

Parametric types in DATs impose a flexible, partial representational structure onto episodes, so that different perspectives on the same episode can simultaneously be maintained. This could be taken to constitute a perspectival variant of the naturalized theory of meaning in Situation Semantics advocated by Barwise and Perry (1983).[3] DAT representations do not depart in any important way from the fundamental tenets of Situation Theory. DAT representations are entirely compatible with the view Barwise and Perry (1985) defend as Aristotelian realism—the view that the natural world is the source of all the structure there is. As language users we are part of the world, we act in the world, and we get information about it by our actions. The perspectival semantic realism underlying the account of dynamic interpretation in this book also locates meaning in the world. Information about the world flows only by our interactions with it, because of our fundamental capacity to use language to communicate information about situations we are not part of. But actions take time and the world changes constantly. The real juggling act we apparently perform with such ease in interpreting natural language consists of matching our linguistic actions with the flow of time, creating a flow of information about our perpetually changing environment. In issuing information, we impose a web onto the world, classifying it into parts that are more or less stable under acquisition of more information. The web of meaningful relations arises because we describe some parts of the world as stable objects, individuals, and plugs. Any change internal to them may safely be ignored for the purposes of the efficient exchange of information. Our use of language therefore depends on our ability to detect, but also disregard, structure in the world. Most things in the world interact quite independently of our descriptions of it. This constrains to an important extent what information the expressions of our language may be used to convey. Any vital semantic theory acknowledges this mutual dependence between communicative action in language and what is happening, in order to maintain a fundamental distinction between change in the world and change in meaning.

7.3 Naturalized Semantic Realism and Universal Grammar

This book has been intended to contribute to a larger research program to develop a linguistically satisfactory theory of how information is encoded and decoded in natural language. In such a dynamic theory the interpretation of a particular use of a sentence is the process of incorporating its informative content into the information already given to the interpreter. Using the same grammatical string in different situations carries different information and hence affects the context in which it is interpreted differently. The content of the string *I am almost done* differs depending on whether I say it, or you do. But not only do such clearly context-dependent expressions as the indexical *I* vary their contribution to the informative content from context to context; as this book has shown, any use of an inflected clause is at least informationally dependent on the very act of using it. The aspectual properties of the simple past, past progressive, and perfect indicate how the information the clause carries is related to its user and how he intends what he describes to be regarded. Aspectual information indicates what the descriptive information he issues is intended to refer to. Modality, counterfactuals, plain conditionals, and generic information, as well as ordinary quantificational sentences—all stickers in DATs—may also be interpreted as having variable content that depends on context, portability conditions, and other background assumptions.[4]

The purpose of this book has been to design a system of reliable rules to extract temporal information about what happened from our natural-language descriptions of it and to reason with such partial information. The resulting system captures the regularities in our linguistic use of English to describe our past. Meaning has been attributed to linguistic expressions by making explicit how they may be used, if we want to convey information about what happened and reason with such linguistically coded information. Relating linguistic expressions to actions by such semantic rules is like using a map, or perhaps a set of related maps with different scales, of the region in which we act. We use the map to guide our actions, trusting that it correctly reflects structural properties of the situation we are in. We can only decide what to do and how to act if we assume first of all that the map is one of this region and second, trust that it is reliable, that it matches the aspects of the world that are relevant to our ways of acting. Of course, many properties of the region are not represented on the map, if it is to be of any practical use. For instance, the actual color of the grass, as an aspect of the situation irrelevant to our communicative purpose, is not encoded on the map, nor does the map indicate where we are now. But the map supposedly represents the way the roads run in virtue of its being a record of the actions, measurements, and findings of its makers. We trust it is an accurate and reliable representation of the way things are in using it to guide our own actions. The rules of DAT representation together form a similar map of our linguistic actions, reflecting, if they are correct, our communal beliefs that a speaker who plays by these rules wants to be understood the same way everyone else is. The rules do not say anything about what it means when a speaker decides to act differently in using her language. They give no guidelines about how to act in situations where the rules are not applied correctly. Furthermore, the rules, realistically, leave plenty of room for our only too common misunderstandings and errors of interpretation. Interpretation is an indeterministic and open-ended process that can run off its track, because of many types of causal interference. One important source of possible misunderstandings is the indeterminacy inherent in the interpretation process, when it requires the interpreter to decide among options. Such choices in the process of interpretation are limited by our prior surveying and recognition of the open options in a given situation. Semantic laziness, ignorance, lack of information or time, fear or other emotions, but also simply myopic vision and limited imagination are among the many ways an interpreter's survey of interpretive options may be restricted, causing potential misunderstandings and often worse.

If our interactions with the world make information about it flow, how is the characteristic human ability to communicate information in a natural language acquired? What is given to a neonate language learner is his environment, including his linguistic community, his bodily experience in situations, and the neurobiological constraints on the functioning of his brain. Humans are naturally disposed to pick up regularities of the situations they are in, in order to make any sense of what is happening. We have a natural tendency to generalize from our immediate experiences in order to determine what to do next and how to guide our future actions. Our will to make sense of what is happening is driven by our will to act. Linguistic abilities unfold as part of the cognitive skills humans developed to survive and to get along in the world, to act meaningfully, and to make sense of what others do. We learn to attribute meaning to what others say, by first seeing how it relates to the situations we are in and gradually understanding how it should relate to situations that we could be in, or have been in. The ability to encode thoughts, observations, and feelings that we want to express in a linguistic medium is first grounded in immediate correlations between sounds and smells, our physical condition, and parts of the world. Our biological limitations help us to forget or ignore certain particularities of the situations we are in, and to select only those that recur and appear useful for constructing meaning. This is required so that we may detect similarities and differences between situations, which leads to the classificatory schemes supported by the language of the community. Learning a first language is part of children's learning how to act, both in comprehension and in production, in order to get other members of the community to understand them. The rules they finally embody in their linguistic practices may contain certain parameters that can be set differently for different languages. This imposes the specific task on linguistic theory of analyzing such parameterization and linguistic variance and of capturing the rules universal to all linguistic systems.

Even if we play by the rules established in our community, there is never any automatic insurance against misunderstandings. In fact, even disregarding the indeterminacy of interpretation, any live linguistic practice still affords considerable room for misunderstanding, for the language and its underlying rule system change continuously. Our linguistic actions require constant monitoring by ourselves and by others, continuous minute adjustments; at the same time we retain our freedom to change a rule of the game at any time or introduce a new one. Our linguistic creativity is one manifestation of the essential indeterminacy of meaning. If we encounter a new linguistic practice in a known language—for example, an isolated new expression or an idiom—or a language we do not know at all, the rules we have already internalized let us determine what unknowns need to be resolved. By seeing repeatedly how information containing the unknown constituents relates to situations in the world, we gradually figure out what they describe. This is again where the fundamental need for parametric types comes in. Parts of our map for linguistic action are temporarily reserved as empty space to be filled in later. But their locations do determine their meaningful relations to objects we have specific information about. The representational flexibility gained by using parametric types allows the linguistic system to determine how the parameters to be resolved are embedded into the described part of the external world. Ignoring this capacity for linguistic creativity so distinctive of human communication embodies a dangerous form of linguistic conservatism. Thinking that mere adjustment of our actions to those of/other community members and a good "fit" between our linguistic actions and the external world guarantees understanding underestimates both our realistic chances for misunderstanding and our fundamental linguistic freedom to act meaningfully in violation of the established rules. A healthy linguistic community not only allows but even promotes as a good survival strategy the necessary tension between fitting in, on the one hand, and innovative, rejuvenating linguistic actions to concoct new meanings, on the other. Our ability to understand such creative use of language, too, is due to the rule-based nature of interpretation. These rules erect such a tightly constructed edifice that we have enough definite hooks and angles to fix meaning and to help us compute the new meaning, even if it is only partial and still subject to revision.

How do we figure out what went wrong when we find that the information on which we based our action does not match the world? What can we do with false information? The difficult task is to determine what part of the available information is in fact deficient in matching the world. That deficiency must be only local, so we need not throw out all the information we have. We still retain most of it to reason toward a conclusion that indicates what to do in order to ensure that we avoid error and maximize the truth of our information in the future. Among the various actions we can take, apart from relying on external authority, is to run experiments to determine truth-values of conclusions that follow from the information we are given. Such "semantic trouble-shooting" eventually narrows down and localizes the false information. All the time we must be alert for possible change of meaning, of course.

The study undertaken in this book to determine how the flow of information encoded in a natural language interacts with the flow of time contributes to our understanding of the constraints on what a possible human linguistic code may be. Such studies capture part of what it takes for a communicative system to be a natural, learnable human language. Among all logically possible languages the natural ones form a small, well-organized class that meet the constraints that arise in part from our inherent biological limitations, and in part from our environmental conditions and our own cognitive states. This account of the flow of information given in natural language is intended to model our semantic competence, the ability all competent speakers of a language share to understand what has been said in any given utterance of an expression of that language. It characterizes *what* contribution a given use of a sentence or expression of another syntactic category makes to the information flow. It makes no claim about *how* this information is obtained by actual mental processing, since this may well vary widely among individual language users. Such *how* claims must be supported by experimentally gained evidence about the behavior of language users on linguistic tasks—a research assignment properly belonging to psycholinguistics and the experimental branches of cognitive science. This study has been theoretical in nature, and linguistic intuitions about meaning and inference have provided its empirical foundation. The results of such theoretical investigations should provide constraints, predictions, and fundamental logical concepts for further experimental research on linguistic practice.

The fundamental distinction was made between interpreting an utterance to determine its informative content and evaluating this information in the external world. The interpretive rules that play a role in determining the information conveyed differ in nature from those that evaluate the information for its truth-value and denotation in a model. The former include rules of inference as operations on the given information that preserve its *assumed* truth. In evaluating information, we determine what it takes for an event to support the type representing the information expressed in an utterance. There was no need for an independently specified and artificial separation between the purely logical vocabulary of the language and its descriptive vocabulary. The fundamental separation was instead between the quantificational apparatus in constraints, the context-changing operations, and the purely descriptive information. This has intentionally blurred the boundaries between the traditional notions of analytical and logical truths. What is considered a necessary truth depends on a host of background assumptions delimiting what alternative states we may consider or what described events are accessible to the evaluation process and inferences. It may simply be harder to keep the meaning of descriptive lexical entries fixed, as a matter of degree, than to keep the meaning of the quantificational apparatus fixed, when conflicting tensions are detected in our linguistic practice.

In the interpretation of natural language I have assumed that uses of inflected clauses describe events, consisting of relations, objects, and polarities. Without an important loss of semantic modeling power, events cannot be reduced to a set of instants with a temporal precedence ordering over them. This nonreductionistic conception of events and states is what makes this system an event-based semantics, providing the basic ontological structure of the intended semantics of the DAT representations. Our capacity to measure time and duration in intervals is derivative on our perception of change in the world. In this event-based system one event is distinguished from another and individuated in the continuously changing world by the types it supports in a given DAT. An event may support a number of different types simultaneously, just as individuals may have many properties at the same time. Since the world does not come prepackaged into events, our linguistic actions partition the continuously changing situation into discrete events, a structured domain about which we report by using the tools of tense and aspect, as well as temporal adverbials and other forms of temporal quantification. If semantic realism locates meaning in the world and causes information to flow from it by our interactions with it, then time is the abstract cognitive category in virtue of which we can bootstrap ourselves from the actual situation we are in and imagine or remember other situations in interpreting our descriptions of what has happened. In such an imagination of our past we may also reinterpret what is happening now. In summary, the view this book has presented holds that in the world surrounding us, however autonomous and solid it may be, we must constantly reconstruct its temporal dimensions and adjust our understanding of what has taken place, depending upon what is actually happening to us now.

Notes

1. Embedded tenses are entirely left out of consideration in this book. Though the sequence-of-tense phenomena constitute very fruitful linguistic territory for semantic study, a proper semantic and logical account of temporal reasoning with tense and aspect in simpler texts is a prerequisite. This is what the current book is designed to accomplish. Like nominal anaphora, temporal anaphora are properly accounted for only if intersentential binding is treated on a par with intrasentential binding of tense.

2. In the terminology used in this book, situations include states and events (cf. "eventualities" in other terminologies). Properly speaking a situation is *classified* by an utterance as belonging to a certain aspectual class, but it is *described* as being of a certain type.

3. Many British speakers seem to prefer a past perfect *had dropped* instead of the simple past in the second sentence of (1.4). This is indeed supported by the account of temporal reference presented in this book (see chapter 4). The point of (1.4) is merely to illustrate that under strong interpretive constraints based on causal connections two simple pasts may be interpreted as the opposite of the textual order. The stative (i)

    (i) The glass is broken. Jane dropped it.

    does not contain the same information as (1.4).

4. Such reverse-order descriptions in the simple past are sometimes considered acceptable when the second clause refers to a preparatory phase of the event described by the first. Webber (1988, 71) argues this point explicitly; also see Moens 1987 and Moens and Steedman 1988. One of Webber's examples is (i).

    (i) John went to the hospital. He took a taxi.

    I would consider taking a taxi part of John's going to the hospital. Hence, Webber's example illustrates the very general case of interpreting two simple pasts as meaning that the first event contains the second one. Clearly the stative *John was at the hospital* requires perfect tense to refer to a previous action that brought that state about, that is, *He had taken a taxi*. If the stative clause is followed by another simple past, *He took a taxi*, then the taxi was taken at the hospital. Webber notes also that reasons for actions (as opposed to causes), do not induce such interpretive constraints allowing the reversal. For example:

    (ii) John went to the hospital. He *broke/had broken his ankle.

5. See Mourelatos 1978 for the Aristotelian division into aspectual classes.

6. See Rooryck and ter Meulen 1992 for arguments against encoding aspectual information in argument structure with a Davidsonian event-argument, as is popular in certain
semantic theories that call themselves "neo-Davidsonian" (e.g., Kratzer 1988, Parsons
1985, 1989, 1990).

7. A very useful contribution to such a cross-linguistic investigation of tense and aspect is
Dahl 1985. Also see Smith 1991 for a comparative account of the semantics of tense
and aspect based on Discourse Representation Theory.

8. A note on the historical significance of choosing the terms *holes, filters,* and *plugs.* The
same three words were introduced for core concepts in the analysis of presupposition
projection by Lauri Karttunen (1973). In Karttunen's work holes allow presuppositions
of their constituent parts to project through entirely (e.g., negation), filters allow only
some presuppositions to project (e.g., conditionals), and plugs block any presupposition
projection (e.g., belief operators). The information-theoretic role that the concepts developed here play in the architecture of temporal representation is different, but not
unrelated. Although this book does not offer a dynamic theory of presupposition projection, such concerns are closely related to the dynamics of context change in tense and
aspect. Such interesting and deep connections between the reference of descriptive information and the projection of presuppositions remain to be discovered in future research.

9. See (1.6)–(1.8) for examples of holes, filters, and plugs, respectively.

10. In chapter 5 an operation on dynamic aspect trees (DATs) is defined, called *perspectival
refinement,* which redefines filters as plugs that may be opened by such refinement. This
avoids the indeterminacy in the interpretation algorithm that is due to filters as defined
here.

11. See Dowty 1979, where causes and completions are essentially tied to inertia worlds,
exotic as they may be, in which "nothing else" changes except that the ongoing event
is completed. Parsons (1990) also relies heavily on such completions or "culminations"
to account for aspectual classes.

12. In truth-conditional semantics "being true twice over" is made precise by requiring that
in a given model there are two variable-assignment functions f and f' that assign
referents to variables, such that each one assigns a different object to *book* (x).

13. Let us not complicate matters even more by considering the situation of buying multiple copies of the same book, despite its obvious relevance to the issue at stake.

14. An episode is a structured set of events described by a DAT. See chapter 3 for a precise
characterization of this notion and its definition.

15. There are interesting issues connected with the interaction of past and future tenses, as
observed by Hornstein (1990, 70).

(i)   a.   *John will leave after Mary arrived.
      b.   John will leave after Mary has arrived.

The future tense is not considered in this book; nor are modalities. But from these data
an initial conjecture seems warranted that future events can only be described as
dependent upon a present perfect state, caused by a future event.

16. See, among others, Kamp 1971, Kaplan 1978, 1979, 1989, and Perry 1977.

17. See ter Meulen 1994b for an analysis of how different kinds of false information may
still be useful.

Chapter 2

1. If the indefiniteness is generalized from the usual weak NPs to the verbal predicates, it
should include verbs like *appear,* and exclude *disappear.* The following extraposition
facts can then be accounted for, by appealing to the symmetry of indefinite relations:

(i) a. There appeared many/*most reviews of this book.
  b. Many/*Most reviews appeared of this book.
  c. *Many reviews disappeared about this book.

See Partee, ter Meulen, and Wall 1990, chapter 13, for background, and Reuland and ter Meulen 1987. These extraposition data were first pointed out to me by Tanya Reinhart in personal communication.

2. In predicate logic the equivalence between, say, *Everyone walks* and *It is not the case that someone does not walk* is captured by the law $\forall x\ \phi \Leftrightarrow \neg\exists x\ \neg\phi$.

3. It is often argued that the quantificational determiners *all*, *every*, and *each* can carry an existential presupposition, requiring their restrictive term to be true. The analogy with the presuppositions of quantificational aspectual verbs may provide additional support for this idea.

4. This point cannot be made with verbs describing actions, since they can be resumed. There also seems some disparity in judgments on these imperative data.

5. The unselective binding of indefinites is observed when a singular indefinite NP in the restrictor of a strong NP is interpreted as having universal force. For example:

(i) Every student who read a book liked it.

This means that every book read by some student or other was liked by him. Other contexts, including conditionals, trigger similar effects. See Kamp and Reyle 1993 and Kamp 1984 for this DRT research. Heim 1982 contains a very similar but independently developed semantics for indefinite NPs with unselective binding. The notion of unselective binding originated in Lewis 1975.

6. DRT accessibility conditions explain why an indefinite NP in the scope of a universal quantifier or some forms of negation, or in conditional contexts, cannot function as an antecedent for anaphora outside that scope or in the continuing context. This is illustrated in (ia–c), where illegitimate binding of a pronoun is indicated by *.

(i) a. Every farmer who owns a donkey feeds it. *It loves the hay.
  b. If a farmer owns a donkey, he feeds it. *It loves the hay.
  c. Jack does not own a donkey. *He feeds it.

See references in note 5. The nature of the interaction between temporal anaphora and nominal anaphora is a key issue for further research. The DATs introduced in chapter 3 substantially constrain the accessibility of NP antecedents for pronouns, depending on the aspectual class of the clause in which they occur.

7. The intrasentential binding restriction has been refined by Roberts (1987) in her analysis of modal subordination in DRT. Another example of such cross-sentential binding in unselective binding contexts is this slight variant on a classic generic example:

(i) Every chess set comes with an extra pawn. It is taped to the side of the box.

Besides modal operators, generic operators allow a subsequent sentence to be incorporated into the nuclear scope in the representation of the sentence preceding it.

8. (2.14) is a slight variant on an example from Freed 1979, an excellent source for intuitions on the semantic behavior of aspectual verbs. Many other interesting differences between *end* and *finish* are discussed there.

9. Remember that *situation* is the generic term for states and events.

10. See Cooper and Kamp 1991 for an extended discussion of various options for the treatment of negation in Situation Semantics and their relation to DRT negation. This paper does not analyze how negation interacts with aspectual classes or with presuppositions. Negation of stative information (e.g., *Jane did not own a car*) should be

represented as states, constraining the dynamic information with a conditional connection between types. Negation of episodic information (e.g., *Jane did not read this book*) is not as strong, but describes the given past situation as a hole, throughout which Jane is not reading.

11. $PROG(T)$ is the type representing clauses with progressive inflection.

12. See Partee, ter Meulen, and Wall 1990, chapter 13, for basic notions and definitions of generalized quantifier theory and their application to NPs.

Chapter 3

1. This way of implementing definiteness is very similar to the familiarity condition in DRT and file-change semantics. See Kamp and Reyle 1993, Heim 1982.

2. See Eggers 1990 for a DRT analysis of temporal anaphora in certain Bantu languages that mark tense only on the first clause of an anaphoric chain. Dahl 1985 contains more data on other languages with similar efficient tense marking.

3. Had the verb been a simple present tense, the type would label the root of the DAT.

4. Again see chapter 6 for the constraint of rigid designation for proper names.

5. Note that there is a real difference between a hole representing Jane's looking at her watch and a sticker that would arise had that information been given using a past progressive. As stickers may be taken along in creating a perspectival shift, if their portability conditions allow it, they are generally harder to pass by than ordinary holes. See chapter 4 regarding the portability conditions on stickers and the progressive.

6. *Inconsistency* means that there is no embedding of the DAT into an event structure; see section 3.4.

7. If nodes x and y have a common ancestor z, then x is a left descendant relative to y iff x is in a chronoscope containing the left branch of some node w that is also contained in the y chronoscope. Of course, z and w may be the same node.

8. Under specific constraints discussed in chapter 4, stickers are transmitted as a DAT grows. They may stick to nodes dominating the node at which they were introduced, if they contain generic or perfective information. Negative states, stickers with a negative polarity expressed as *not yet*, can under certain conditions be transmitted to nodes that precede the node at which they were introduced.

9. We have not yet made any use of roles in DAT representations. They are listed here for sake of completeness of the *TYPE* specification. The additional condition on forming roles from restricted parametric types is called the *absorption law* in Gawron and Peters 1990, supported by empirical linguistic arguments based on VP anaphora.

10. See chapter 6 for such lexical constraints on compatible types.

11. So $\pi_N(n)$ is definable from $\delta_N(n)$.

12. In chapter 5 it will turn out to be necessary to constrain this function to assign non-empty sets of types to the nodes.

13. See van Benthem 1983 for arguments why convexity and monotonicity are the minimal principles governing the event-based temporal logic. Overlap is definable (x overlaps with y iff there is a z that is part of both).

14. The notion c-command (constituent-command) is an adaptation of a core configurational notion in generative syntax. It is defined here as follows: a node n c-commands all right descendants of its parent.

15. Dowty 1979, Bennett and Partee 1978, Hoepelman and Rohrer 1980, and Mourelatos 1978 are some of the older publications concerned with the "imperfective paradox" from which the current discussions ensued.

Chapter 4

1. See chapter 6 for details of their lexical representation.
2. In DRT no semantic distinction is made between activities and states, for they all are represented by requiring their DR marker to include the given reference time. It is nevertheless important for a semantic representation to keep track of the order in which this information is received, if it is to account properly for situated inferences with stative information.
3. These examples may provide a good testing ground for the different predictions one can make with DAT representations and DRT representations. In DRT the current reference time would be included in all four states, but no other relation would obtain between the states, so (4.9), (4.10), and (4.11) would have the same content and would presumably validate the same inferences.
4. See the introduction in Carlson and Pelletier 1994 for this distinction and the extensive linguistic evidence that supports it.
5. See the papers collected in Carlson and Pelletier 1994; my paper in that collection (ter Meulen 1994a) addresses constraints on the anaphoric type-shifting between pronouns and NPs that refer to kinds and their members.
6. Again, see the papers in Carlson and Pelletier 1994 for detailed analyses of how such characteristic-kind-predication statements are to be partitioned into restrictor and nuclear scope.
7. To avoid the additional complications of interpreting the present tense, the illustrations all use the simple past.
8. See Moravcsik 1991 for a discussion of the existential commitments of accidental generalizations expressed in conditionals, like the example (4.19b). Lawlike statements have no such commitment. I share the view defended by Moravcsik that the form of a statement does not indicate whether it is an accidental generalization or a lawlike statement. The existential commitment need not be satisfied by the current node to which the sticker is appended, but should be satisfied by some node in the DAT.
9. See, among others, Stalnaker 1975, Barwise 1986b, Carlson 1982, Cartwright 1989 for further discussion of stable background contexts for conditionals and the *ceteris paribus* clauses of causal laws. Heim 1992 addresses the projection of presuppositions of conditionals and counterfactuals in a dynamic context-change semantics.

Chapter 5

1. Seligman (1990) uses a different notion of perspective. The core issue for a semantic theory that employs such a notion is to characterize what makes a perspective change.
2. The current node need not be a terminal node; for example, while backing up in a chronoscope, the interpreter can plug up a higher node and select it as the current node in order to create a new one later than it.
3. This example depends on the use of the present tense to ensure that the stickers are attached to the root, not to a node in a left chronoscope. Present tense interpretation brings in more problems than this book is designed to deal with; for that reason, it is not included in the fragment in chapter 6. See chapter 4 for the definitions of simple stickers and perfect *PERF* stickers and their associated portability conditions.
4. One objection to DRT is exactly this need to determine verifying embeddings for discourse representations with an "empty" reference time marker that carries no descriptive information, other than the requirement that it be preceded by the old reference time marker. The rule for accomplishments and achievements requires such a condition in the discourse representation. (See, for instance, Hinrichs 1986 and Partee 1984. It remains

unclear how we determine the reference of such an "empty" reference time marker correctly so that information we receive only later is indeed true of it. Mere trial and error seems the only resort—and this means the embeddings may have to be undone, if the chosen time turns out later not to have been the one at which the events described later are indeed happening.

5. Note that a universal aspectual verb such as *keep or continue* would not trigger a flash-back. For example, after (5.5a) the clause *when she continued to call* ... would mean that she returned to the booth and started calling again. See ter Meulen 1991 for other linguistic evidence that only dynamic aspectual verbs trigger flashbacks.

6. Below I substantiate the claim, implicit here, that suitable antecedents of flashbacks are always plugs. This leads to a constraint on the search for antecedents that restricts the search to plugs of past chronoscopes, which need not be terminal nodes.

Chapter 6

1. See Moortgat 1988 for fundamental insights and detailed linguistic arguments showing the advantages of the Lambek systems as grammars for natural language.

2. Jackendoff (1990) represents adverbs as arguments in the verbal projections. My choice to represent them as adjuncts reflects the semantic consideration that they should describe relations between events or properties of events, and not constituents, such as the objects that take part in the event. This view of adverbial modification has been a core claim of Davidson's semantic program (see Davidson 1967, 1980, 1984).

3. In this simple fragment Agr contains the person and number agreement features and is a constituent of Infl. There may be good linguistic arguments to restructure Infl in a more sophisticated syntax according to the "Split Inflection Hypothesis," as has been suggested by Pollock (1989) and Chomsky (1991), but this would lead far beyond the simplifying intentions of this fragment.

4. Stative VPs are lexically marked in this fragment by the lack of an event parameter in their verbal argument structure in the lexicon.

5. See Diesing 1992 for arguments based on German scrambling contexts, supporting the claim that only in generic IPs is the subject NP generated in Spec IP. Diesing's analysis is closely related to the issues discussed in chapter 4, but DATs provide much more structural context for the restrictor than do ordinary linear LF representations of clauses.

6. This section owes its existence to some instructive discussions with Michael Moortgat on the connection between generative syntax and Lambek grammars. Moortgat 1988 and 1993 constitute the basis for the exposition in this section.

7. Gawron and Peters (1990) do represent tense as an argument of the verbal projection. They not only attempt to represent the context-change potential of tense and aspect in the types, but also mix in all kinds of semantic conditions (uniqueness of referents, instances of parameters, scope relations, resource situations contained in the context, etc.). DAT representations intentionally separate the descriptive information repre-sented in types from the control information determining the architecture of DAT representations.

8. See van Benthem 1983 for arguments why convexity and monotonicity are the minimal principles governing the event-based temporal logic. Overlap is definable (x overlaps with y iff there is a z that is part of both).

9. $\pi_N(n)$ is the parent node of n in the set of nodes N of the DAT.

10. Where V_a abbreviates the categories of auxiliary and attitude verbs.

11. The puzzle was brought to my attention by Jackendoff (1983).

Chapter 7

1. Johan van Benthem and Jerry Seligman have suggested in personal communication that a modal logic equivalent to DAT representation should have four-place operators, even if unplugging in perspectival refinement is left out of consideration.
2. The truth-functional paradoxes that may seem to threaten systems with circularity in semantics should be resolvable along the lines suggested by Barwise and Etchemendy (1987), giving a Situation-Theoretic account based on non-well-founded sets.
3. Seligman (1990) characterizes a notion of perspective in Situation Theory. Several other papers in Situation Theory use a notion of perspective as well, but they may capture different concepts, and they certainly use it for different purposes.
4. Robert Stalnaker equates the context + background assumptions with the "common ground" of the information exchange. See Stalnaker 1978, 1984.

Bibliography

Allen, J. F. 1984. Towards a general theory of action and time. *Artificial Intelligence* 23, 123–154.

Almeida, M. J. 1987. Reasoning about the temporal structure of narratives. Ph.D. dissertation, State University of New York, Buffalo.

Anscombe, G. 1964. Before and after. *Philosophical Review* 73, 3–24.

Asher, N. 1992. A default, truth conditional semantics for the progressives. *Linguistics and Philosophy* 15, 463–508.

Bach, E. 1981. On time, tense and aspect: An essay in English metaphysics. In P. Cole, ed., *Radical pragmatics*, 63–81. New York: Academic Press.

Bach, E. 1986a. The algebra of events. *Linguistics and Philosophy* 91, 5–17.

Bach, E. 1986b. Natural language metaphysics. In R. B. Marcus, G. J. W. Dorn, and P. Weingartner, eds., *Logic, methodology, and philosophy of science* 7, 573–595. Amsterdam: North-Holland.

Banfield, A. 1982. *Unspeakable sentences: Narration and representation in the language of fiction.* London: Routledge & Kegan Paul.

Bartsch, R. 1972. The syntax and semantics of number and numbers. In J. Kimball, ed., *Syntax and semantics 2*, 51–94. New York: Academic Press.

Bartsch, R. 1976. *The grammar of adverbials.* New York: North-Holland.

Bartsch, R. 1986. On aspectual properties of Dutch and German nominalizations. In Lo Cascio and Vet 1986, 7–40.

Bartsch, R. 1989. Tense and aspect in discourse. *Theoretical Linguistics* 15:1/2, 133–194.

Barwise, J. 1981. Scenes and other situations. *Journal of Philosophy* 78, 369–397.

Barwise, J. 1986a. Noun phrases, generalized quantifiers and anaphora. In P. Gårdenfors, ed., *Generalized quantifiers,* 1–29. Dordrecht: Reidel.

Barwise, J. 1986b. Conditionals and conditional information. In E. Traugott, A. G. B. ter Meulen, J. Reilly, and C. Ferguson, (eds), *On conditionals,* 21–54. Cambridge: Cambridge University Press.

Barwise, J. 1989. The situation in logic. CSLI Lecture Notes 17, Stanford University. Distributed by University of Chicago Press.

Barwise, J., and R. Cooper. 1981. Generalized quantifiers and natural language. *Linguistics and Philosophy* 4, 159–219.

Barwise, J., and J. Etchemendy. 1987. *The liar: An essay in truth and circularity.* Oxford: Oxford University Press.

Barwise, J., and J. Perry. 1983. *Situations and attitudes.* Cambridge. Mass.: MIT Press.

Barwise, J., and J. Perry. 1985. Interview. *Linguistics and Philosophy* 8, 105–161.

Bäuerle, R. 1979. *Temporale Deixis, temporale Frage.* Tübingen: Gunter Narr Verlag.

Bäuerle, R. 1987. *Ereignisse und Repräsentationen.* Habilitationsschrift, Universität Konstanz.

Bäuerle, R., U. Egli, and A. von Stechow, eds. 1979. *Semantics from different points of view.* Berlin: Springer-Verlag.

Bäuerle, R., C. Schwartze, and A. von Stechow, eds. 1983. *Meaning, use, and interpretation of language.* Berlin: de Gruyter.

Bellert, I. 1977. On semantic and distributional properties of sentential adverbs. *Linguistic Inquiry* 8, 337–351.

Bennett, J. 1988. *Events and their names.* Indianapolis, Ind.: Hackett Press.

Bennett, M. 1977. A guide to the logic of tense and aspect in English. *Logique et analyse* 20, 491–517.

Bennett, M. 1979. Mass nouns and mass terms in Montague Grammar. In Davis and Mithun 1979, 263–286.

Bennett, M. 1981. Of tense and aspect: One analysis. In Tedeschi and Zaenen 1981, 13–30.

Bennett, M., and B. Partee. 1978. *Toward the logic of tense and aspect in English.* Bloomington, Ind.: Indiana University Linguistics Club.

Bryan, R. 1980. Elements of an improved treatment of tense, aspect and temporal deixis in a Montague framework. Ph. D. dissertation, University of Kansas.

Caenepeel, M., and G. Sandström. 1992. A discourse-level approach to the past perfect in narrative. In M. Aurnague, A. Borillo, M. Borillo, and M. Bras, eds., *Proceedings of the Bonas Workshop,* 167–182. IRIT, Université Paul Sabatier, Toulouse.

Carlson, G. 1977. A unified analysis of the English bare plural. *Linguistics and Philosophy* 1, 413–458.

Carlson, G. 1980. *Reference to kinds in English.* New York: Garland.

Carlson, G. 1982. Generic terms and generic sentences. *Journal of Philosophical Logic* 11, 145–182.

Carlson, G., and J. Pelletier, eds. 1994. *The generic book.* Chicago: University of Chicago Press.

Cartwright, H. 1975. Some remarks about mass nouns and plurality. *Synthese* 31, 395–410.

Cartwright, N. 1989. *Nature's capacities and their measurement.* Oxford: Clarendon Press.

Chomsky, N. 1970. Remarks on nominalization. In R. Jacobs and P. Rosenbaum, eds., *Readings in English transformational grammar,* 184–221. Waltham, Mass.: Ginn.

Chomsky, N. 1991. Some notes on economy of derivation and representation. In R. Freidin, ed., *Principles and parameters in comparative grammar,* 417–454. Cambridge, Mass.: MIT Press.

Clark, H. 1973. Space, time, semantics and the child. In T. E. Moore, ed., *Cognitive development and the acquisition of language,* 27–63. New York: Academic Press.

Cocchiarella, N. 1979. The theory of homogeneous simple types as second order logic. *Notre Dame Journal of Formal Logic* 20, 505–524.

Comrie, B. 1976. *Aspect: An introduction to the study of verbal aspect and related problems.* Cambridge: Cambridge University Press.

Comrie, B. 1985. *Tense.* Cambridge: Cambridge University Press.

Cooper, R. 1985. Aspectual classes in Situation Semantics. CSLI Report 84-14C, Stanford University.

Cooper, R. 1986. Tense and discourse location in Situation Semantics. *Linguistics and Philosophy* 9, 17–36.

Cooper, R., and H. Kamp. 1991. Negation in Situation Semantics and Discourse Representation Theory. In J. Barwise, J. M. Gawron, G. Plotkin, and S. Tutiya, eds., *Situation Theory and its applications, vol. 2,* 311–334. CSLI Lecture Notes 26, Stanford University. Distributed by University of Chicago Press.

Cresswell, M. 1985a. *Structured meanings: The semantics of propositional attitudes.* Cambridge, Mass.: MIT Press.

Cresswell, M. 1985b. *Adverbial modification.* Dordrecht: Reidel.

Dahl, Ö. 1985. *Tense and aspect systems*. Oxford: Blackwell.

Davidson, D. 1967. The logical form of action sentences. In N. Rescher, ed., *The logic of decision and action*, 81–95. Pittsburgh, Penn.: University of Pittsburgh Press. Reprinted in Davidson 1980, 106–148.

Davidson, D. 1980. *Essays on actions and events*. Oxford: Clarendon Press.

Davidson, D. 1984. *Inquiries into truth and interpretation*. Oxford: Clarendon Press.

Davidson, D., and G. Harman, eds. 1972. *Semantics of natural language*. Dordrecht: Reidel.

Davis, S., and M. Mithun, eds. 1979. *Linguistics, philosophy and Montague Grammar*. Austin, Tex.: University of Texas Press.

DeClerck, R. 1991. *Tense in English: Its structure and use in discourse*. London: Routledge.

de Groot, C., and H. Tommola, eds. 1984. *Aspect bound: A voyage into the realm of Germanic, Slavonic and Finno-Ugrian aspectology*. Dordrecht: Foris.

Diesing, M. 1992. Bare plural subjects and the derivation of logical representations. *Linguistic Inquiry* 23, 353–380.

Dowty, D. 1979. *Word meaning and Montague Grammar*. Dordrecht: Reidel.

Dowty, D. 1982. Tenses, time adverbials and compositional semantic theory. *Linguistics and Philosophy* 5, 23–58.

Dowty, D. 1986. The effects of aspectual class on the temporal structure of discourse: Semantics or pragmatics? *Linguistics and Philosophy* 9, 37–61.

Eggers, E. 1990. Temporal anaphora in discourse. Ph.D. dissertation, University of Washington.

Emonds, J. E. 1985. *A unified theory of syntactic categories*. Dordrecht: Foris.

Enç, M. 1981. Tense without scope: An analysis of nouns as indexicals. Ph.D. dissertation, University of Wisconsin.

Enç, M. 1986. Towards a referential analysis of temporal expressions. *Linguistics and Philosophy* 9, 405–426.

Enç, M. 1987. Anchoring conditions for tense. *Linguistic Inquiry* 18, 633–657.

Fenstad, J.-E., K. Halvorsen, T. Langholm, and J. van Benthem. 1987. *Situations, language and logic*. Dordrecht: Reidel.

Freed, A. 1979. *The semantics of English aspectual complementation*. Dordrecht: Reidel.

Frege, G. 1892. On sense and reference. In P. Geach and M. Black, eds., *Translations from the philosophical writings of Gottlob Frege*, 56–78. Oxford: Blackwell, 1952.

Galton, A. 1984. *The logic of aspect: An axiomatic approach*. Oxford: Clarendon Press.

Galton, A., ed. 1987. *Temporal logics and their applications*. New York: Academic Press.

Gawron, J. M. 1986. Types, contents and semantic objects. *Linguistics and Philosophy* 9, 427–476.

Gawron, J. M., and S. Peters. 1990. *Anaphora and quantification in Situation Semantics*. CSLI Lecture Notes 19, Stanford University. Distributed by: University of Chicago Press.

Geach, P. 1962. *Reference and generality*. Ithaca, N.Y. Cornell University Press.

Goldblatt, R. 1987. *Logics of time and computation*. CSLI Lecture Notes 7, Stanford University. Distributed by University of Chicago Press.

Glasbey, S. 1993. Event structure in natural language discourse. Ph.D. dissertation, University of Edinburgh.

Grätzer, G. 1971. *Lattice-theory: First concepts and distributive lattices*. San Francisco: Freeman.

Gruber, J. 1976. *Lexical structures in syntax and semantics*. Amsterdam: North-Holland.

Günthner, F., C. Habel, and C. R. Rollinger. 1983. Ereignisnetze: Zeitnetze und referentielle Netze. *Linguistische Berichte* 88, 37–55.

Günthner, F., and C. Rohrer, eds. 1978. *Studies in formal semantics: Intensionality, temporality, negation*. Amsterdam: North-Holland.

Günthner, F., and S. Schmidt, eds. 1979. *Formal semantics and pragmatics for natural languages*. Dordrecht: Reidel.

Hacking, I. 1979. What is logic? *Journal of Philosophy* 76, 285–319.

Hayes, P. 1979. The naive physics manifesto. In D. Mitchie, ed., *Expert systems in the microelectronic age*, 242–270. Edinburgh: Edinburgh University Press.

Heim, I. 1982. The semantics of definite and indefinite noun-phrases. Ph.D. dissertation, University of Massachusetts, Amherst. New York: Garland.

Heim, I. 1992. Presupposition projection and the semantics of attitude verbs. *Journal of Semantics* 9, 183–221.

Heinämäki, O. 1983. Aspect in Finnish. In de Groot and Tommola 1984, 153–177.

Hinrichs, E. 1981. Temporale Anaphora im Englischen. Magister arbeit, Universität Tübingen.

Hinrichs, E. 1983. The semantics of the English progressive. In *CLS 19: Papers from the Nineteenth Regional Meeting*, 171–182. Chicago Linguistic Society, University of Chicago.

Hinrichs, E. 1985. A compositional semantics for Aktionsarten and NP reference in English. Ph.D. dissertation, Ohio State University.

Hinrichs, E. 1986. Temporal anaphora in discourses of English. *Linguistics and Philosophy* 9, 63–82.

Hinrichs, E. 1988. Tense, quantifiers, and contexts. *Computational Linguistics* 14.2, 3–14.

Hintikka, J., J. Moravcsik, and P. Suppes, eds. 1973. *Approaches to natural language*. Dordrecht: Reidel.

Hoepelman, J., and C. Rohrer. 1980. On the mass-count distinction and the French imparfait and passé simple. In Rohrer 1980, 85–112.

Hopper, P. 1982. *Tense, aspect between semantics and pragmatics*. Amsterdam: W. Benjamins.

Hornstein, N. 1990. *As time goes by*. Cambridge, Mass.: MIT Press.

Jackendoff, R. 1983. *Semantics and cognition*. Cambridge, Mass.: MIT Press.

Jackendoff, R. 1987. The status of thematic relations in linguistic theory. *Linguistic Inquiry* 18, 369–411.

Jackendoff, R. 1990. *Semantic structures*. Cambridge, Mass.: MIT Press.

Jackendoff, R. 1991. Parts and boundaries. *Cognition* 41, 9–45.

Jakobson, R. 1957. Shifters, verbal categories, and the Russian verb. In *Selected writings*, 130–147. The Hague: Mouton.

Jarvis Thomson, J. 1977. *Acts and other events*. Ithaca, N.Y.: Cornell University Press.

Jarvis Thomson, J. 1983. Parthood and identity across time. *Journal of Philosophy* 80, 201–220.

Kamp, H. 1968. Tense logic and the theory of linear order. Ph.D. dissertation, University of California, Los Angeles.

Kamp, H. 1971. Formal properties of "now." *Theoria* 37, 227–273.

Kamp, H. 1979. Events, instants and temporal reference. In Bäuerle, Egli, and von Stechow 1979, 376–417.

Kamp, H. 1980. Some remarks on the logic of change. In Rohrer 1980, 135–179.

Kamp, H. 1981. Evénements, représentations discursives et référence temporelle. *Langages* 64, 39–64.

Kamp, H. 1984. A theory of truth and semantic representation. In J. Groenendijk, M. Stokhof, and T. Janssen, eds., *Truth, interpretation and information*, 1–41. Dordrecht: Foris. (original from 1981)

Kamp, H., and U. Reyle. 1993. *From discourse to logic*. Dordrecht: Kluwer.

Kamp, H., and C. Rohrer. 1983. Tense in texts. In: Bäuerle, Schwartze, and von Stechow 1983, 250–269.

Kaplan, D. 1978. Dthat. In P. Cole, ed., *Syntax and semantics* 9, 221–243. New York: Academic Press.

Kaplan, D. 1979. On the logic of demonstratives. *Journal of Philosophical Logic* 8, 81–98. Reprinted in N. Salmon and S. Soames, eds. 1988. *Propositions and attitudes*, 66–82. New York: Oxford University Press.

Kaplan, D. 1989. Demonstratives: An essay on the semantics, logic, metaphysics and epistemology of demonstratives and other indexicals. In J. Almog, J. Perry, and H. Wettstein, eds., *Themes from Kaplan*, 481–563. New York: Oxford University Press.

Karttunen, L. 1973. Presuppositions of compound sentences. *Linguistic Inquiry* 4, 169–193.

Klooster, W. 1972. *The structure underlying measure phrase sentences*. Dordrecht: Reidel.

Kratzer, A. 1988. Stage and individual level predication. In M. Krifka, ed., *Genericity in natural language: Proceedings of a Tübingen conference*, 247–284. Also in Carlson and Pelletier 1994.

Kratzer, A. 1989. Lumps of thought. *Linguistics and Philosophy* 12, 607–653.

Krifka, M. 1986. Nominalreferenz und Zeitkonstitution: Zur Semantik von Massentermen, Pluraltermen und Aspektklassen. Dissertation, Ludwig Maximilians Universität München.

Krifka, M. 1987. Nominal reference and temporal constitution: Towards a semantics of quantity. In J. Groenendijk, M. Stokhof, and F. Veltman, eds., *Proceedings of the 6th Amsterdam Colloquium*, 153–173. ITaLI, University of Amsterdam.

Kripke, S. 1980. *Naming and necessity*. Cambridge, Mass.: Harvard University Press.

Lamiroy, B. 1987. The complementation of aspectual verbs in French. *Language* 63, 278–298.

Lasersohn, P. 1990. Group action and spatio-temporal proximity. *Linguistics and Philosophy* 13, 179–206.

LePore, E., and B. McLaughlin, eds. 1985. *Actions and events: Perspectives on the philosophy of Donald Davidson*. Oxford: Blackwell.

Lewis, D. 1975. Adverbs of quantification. In E. Keenan, ed., *Formal semantics of natural language*, 3–15. Cambridge: Cambridge University Press.

Lewis, D. 1986. Events. In *Philosophical papers*, vol. 2, 241–270. Oxford: Oxford University Press.

Link, G. 1983. The logical analysis of plurals and mass terms: A lattice-theoretical approach. In Bäuerle, Schwartze, and von Stechow 1983, 302–323.

Link, G. 1987a. Algebraic semantics for event structures. In J. Groenendijk, M. Stokhof, and F. Veltman, eds., *Proceedings of the 6th Amsterdam Colloquium*, 243–262. ITaLI, University of Amsterdam.

Link, G. 1987b. Generalized quantifiers and plurals. In P. Gårdenfors, ed., *Generalized quantifiers: Logical and linguistic approaches*, 151–180. Dordrecht: Kluwer.

Lo Cascio, V., and C. Vet, eds. 1986. *Temporal structure in sentence and discourse*. Dordrecht: Foris.

Löbner, S. 1987. Ansätze zu einer integralen semantische Theorie von Tempus, Aspekt und Aktionsarten. In V. Ehrich and H. Vater, eds., *Temporalsemantik*, 163–191. Tübingen: Max Niemeyer Verlag.

Lønning, J. T. 1987. Mass terms and quantification. *Linguistics and Philosophy* 10, 1–52.

McCawley, J. D. 1971. Tense and time reference in English. In C. Fillmore and T. Langendoen, eds., *Studies in linguistic semantics*, 96–113. New York: Holt, Rinehart and Winston.

McCoard, J. 1978. *The English perfect: Tense-choice and pragmatic inferences*. Amsterdam: North-Holland.

McDermott, D. 1982. A temporal logic for reasoning about processes and plans. *Cognitive Science* 6, 101–155.

Moens, M. 1987. Tense, aspect and temporal reference. Ph.D. dissertation, University of Edinburgh.

Moens, M., and M. Steedman. 1988. Temporal ontology and temporal reference. *Computational Linguistics* 14.2, 15–28.

Montague, R. 1974. *Formal philosophy*. R. Thomason, ed. New Haven, Conn.: Yale University Press.

Moortgat, M. 1988. *Categorial investigations: Logical and linguistic aspects of the Lambek calculus*. Reprinted in 1992. Berlin: de Gruyter.

Moortgat, M. 1993. The logic of heads. Notes for a workshop in Logic, Language and Computation, CSLI, Stanford University.

Moravçsik, J. 1991. "All A's are B's": Form and content. *Journal of Pragmatics* 16, 427–441.

Mourelatos, A. 1978. Events, states and processes. *Linguistics and Philosophy* 2/3, 415–434.

Mourelatos, A. 1981. Events, processes, and states. In: Tedeschi and Zaenen 1981, 191–212.

Nakhimovsky, A. 1988. Aspect, aspectual class, and the temporal structure of narrative. *Computational Linguistics* 14.2, 29–43.

Nelson, K. 1986. *Event knowledge: Structure and function in development*. Hillsdale N.J.: Erlbaum.

Newmeyer, F. 1975. *English aspectual verbs*. The Hague: Mouton.

Parsons, T. 1985. Underlying events in the logical analysis of English. In LePore and McLaughlin 1985, 235–267.

Parsons, T. 1989. The progressive in English: Events, states and processes. *Linguistics and Philosophy* 12, 213–241.

Parsons, T. 1990. *Events in the semantics of English: A study in subatomic semantics*. Cambridge, Mass.: MIT Press.

Partee, B. 1973. Some structural analogies between tenses and pronouns in English. *The Journal of Philosophy* 70, 601–609.

Partee, B., ed. 1976. *Montague Grammar*. New York: Academic Press.

Partee, B. 1984. Nominal and temporal anaphora. *Linguistics and Philosophy* 7, 243–286.

Partee, B., A. G. B. ter Meulen, and R. Wall. 1990. *Mathematical methods in linguistics*. Dordrecht: Kluwer.

Passonneau, R. 1988. A computational model of the semantics of tense and aspect. *Computational Linguistics* 14.2, 44–60.

Pelletier, J. 1979. *Mass terms: Some philosophical problems*. Dordrecht: Reidel.

Perlmutter, D. 1970. The two verbs "begin." In R. Jacobs and P. Rosenbaum, eds., *Readings in English transformational grammar*, 107–119. Waltham, Mass.: Ginn.

Perry, J. 1977. Frege on demonstratives. *Philosophical Review* 86, 474–497.

Platzack, C. 1979. *The semantic interpretation of aspect and Aktionsarten: A study of internal time reference in Swedish*. Dordrecht: Foris.

Pollock, J.-Y. 1989. Verb movement, Universal Grammar, and the structure of IP. *Linguistic Inquiry* 20, 365–424.

Prior, A. 1967. *Past, present and future*. Oxford: Oxford University Press.

Pustejovsky, J. 1991. The syntax of event-structure. *Cognition* 41, 47–81.

Reichenbach, H. 1947. *Elements of symbolic logic*. New York: Academic Press.

Reuland, E., and A. G. B. ter Meulen, eds. 1987. *The representation of (in)definiteness*. Cambridge, Mass.: MIT Press.

Reyle, U. 1986. Zeit und Aspekt bei der Verarbeitung natürlicher Sprachen. Dr. Phil. dissertation, Universität Stuttgart.

Roberts, C. 1987. Modal subordination, anaphora and distributivity. Ph.D. dissertation, University of Massachusetts, Amherst. Published by Garland, New York.

Rohrer, C., ed. 1977. *On the logical analysis of tense and aspect*. Tübingen: Günter Narr Verlag.

Rohrer, C. ed. 1980. *Time, tense and quantifiers*. Tübingen: Max Niemeyer Verlag.

Rohrer, C. 1986. Indirect discourse and "Consecutio Temporum." In Lo Cascio and Vet 1986, 79–98.

Rooryck, J., and A. G. B. ter Meulen. 1992. The quantificational force of static and dynamic predication. In D. Bates, ed., *Proceedings of the Tenth West Coast Conference on Formal Linguistics*, 459–470. CSLI, Stanford University. Distributed by University of Chicago Press.

Schubert, L., and C. H. Hwang. 1990. *An episodic knowledge representation for narrative texts.* Technical Report 345, Computer Science, University of Rochester.

Seligman, J. 1990. Perspectives in Situation Theory. In R. Cooper, K. Mukai, and J. Perry, eds., *Situation theory and its applications, vol. 1*, 147–192. CSLI Lecture Notes 22, Stanford University. Distributed by University of Chicago Press.

Seligman, J., and A. G. B. ter Meulen. 1992. Dynamic aspect trees. In K. Bimbo, ed., *Proceedings of the Third Workshop on Logic and Linguistics*, 199–234. Hungarian Academy of Sciences, Budapest.

Siegel, M. 1979. Measure adjectives in Montague Grammar. In Davis and Mithun 1979, 223–262.

Siegel, M. 1987. Compositionality, case and the scope of auxiliaries. *Linguistics and Philosophy* 10, 53–75.

Smessaert, H. 1993. The logical geometry of comparison and quantification. Ph.D. dissertation, University of Leuven.

Smith, C. 1978. The syntax and interpretation of temporal reference in English. *Linguistics and Philosophy* 2, 43–100.

Smith, C. 1981. Semantic and syntactic constraints on temporal interpretation. In Tedeschi and Zaenen 1981, 213–237.

Smith, C. 1986. A speaker-based approach to aspect. *Linguistics and Philosophy* 9, 97–115.

Smith, C. 1991. *The parameter of aspect.* Dordrecht: Kluwer.

Stalnaker, R. 1972. Pragmatics. In: Davidson and Harman 1972, 280–397.

Stalnaker, R. 1973. Presuppositions. *Journal of Philosophical Logic* 2, 447–457.

Stalnaker, R. 1975. Indicative conditionals. *Philosophia* 5, 269–286.

Stalnaker, R. 1978. Assertion. In P. Cole, ed., *Syntax and semantics 9*, 315–332. New York: Academic Press.

Stalnaker, R. 1984. *Inquiry.* Cambridge, Mass.: MIT Press.

Steedman, M. 1982. Reference to past time. In R. Jarvella and W. Klein, eds., *Speech, place and action*, 125–157. New York: Wiley.

Tedeschi, P., and A. Zaenen, eds. 1981. *Tense and aspect.* New York: Academic Press.

Tenny, C. L. 1992. Aspectual roles and the syntax-semantics interface. Ms., University of Pittsburgh.

ter Meulen, A. G. B. 1980. Substances, quantities and individuals: A study in the formal semantics of mass terms. Ph.D. dissertation, Stanford University.

ter Meulen, A. G. B. 1981. An intensional logic for mass terms. *Philosophical Studies* 40, 105–125. Reprinted with revisions in J. Groenendijk, M. Stokhof, and T. Janssen, eds., *Formal methods in the study of language*, 421–444. Mathematical Centre Tract 135. Amsterdam.

ter Meulen, A. G. B. 1984. Events, quantities and individuals. In F. Landman and F. Veltman, eds., *Varieties of formal semantics*, 259–280. Dordrecht: Foris.

ter Meulen, A. G. B. 1985a. Progressives without possible worlds. In W. H. Eilfort, P. D. Kroeber, and K. L. Peterson, eds., *CLS 21*, part 1, 408–423. Chicago Linguistic Society, University of Chicago.

ter Meulen, A. G. B. 1985b. Homogeneous and individuated quantifiers in natural language. In P. Weingartner and G. Dorn, eds., *Foundations of logic and linguistics*, 543–562. New York: Plenum.

ter Meulen, A. G. B. 1986a. Generic information, conditional contexts and constraints. In
E. Traugott, A. G. B. ter Meulen, J. Reilly, and C. Ferguson, eds. *On conditionals*,
123–146. Cambridge: Cambridge University Press.

ter Meulen, A. G. B. 1986b. Structured domains for events. *Journal of Symbolic Logic* 51, 857
(abstract).

ter Meulen, A. G. B. 1987a. Locating events. In J. Groenendijk and M. Stokhof, eds.,
Foundations of pragmatics and lexical semantics, 27–40. Dordrecht: Foris.

ter Meulen, A. G. B. 1987b. Incomplete events. In J. Groenendijk, M. Stokhof, and F.
Veltman, eds., *Proceedings of the 6th Amsterdam Colloquium*, 263–279. ITaLI, University of Amsterdam.

ter Meulen, A. G. B. 1990. English aspectual verbs as generalized quantifiers. In J. Carter,
R.-M. Déchaine, B. Philip, and T. Sherer, eds., *Proceedings of NELS 20*, 378–390.
GLSA, University of Massachusetts, Amherst. Also in *Proceedings of the 7th
Amsterdam Colloquium, vol. 1*, 303–315. ITaLI, University of Amsterdam; and with
revisions in A. L. Halpern, ed., *The Proceedings of the Ninth West Coast Conference on
Formal Linguistics*, 347–360. CSLI, Stanford University. Distributed by University of
Chicago Press.

ter Meulen, A. G. B. 1991. Shifting of reference time and perspective. In L. A. Sutton, C.
Johnson, and R. Shields, eds., *Proceedings of the Seventeenth Annual Meeting of the
Berkeley Linguistics Society*, 520–530. Berkeley Linguistics Society, University of California, Berkeley.

ter Meulen, A. G. B. 1992. How to preserve information in a dynamic environment: Trees
for temporal reasoning. In M. Aurnague, A. Borillo, M. Borillo, and M. Bras, eds.,
Proceedings of the Bonas Workshop, 309–323. IRIT, Université Paul Sabatier, Toulouse.

ter Meulen, A. G. B. 1994a. Semantic constraints on type-shifting anaphora. In Carlson and
Pelletier 1994.

ter Meulen, A. G. B. 1994b. Demonstrations, indications and experiments. *The Monist* 77,
239–256.

Thomason, J. J. 1971. Individuating actions. *Journal of Philosophy* 68, 771–781.

Tichy, P. 1980. The logic of temporal discourse. *Linguistics and Philosophy* 3, 343–369.

Ullmer-Ehrich, V. 1977. Zur Syntax und Semantik von Substantivierungen im Deutschen.
Kronberg: Skriptor Verlag.

van Benthem, J. 1983. The logic of time. Dordrecht: Reidel.

van Benthem, J. 1991. Temporal logic. In D. Gabbay, C. Hogger, and J. Robinson, eds.,
Handbook of logic in computer science, 241–348. Oxford: Oxford University Press.

Vendler, Z. 1967. *Linguistics in philosophy*. Ithaca, N.Y.: Cornell University Press.

Vendler, Z. 1984. Agency and causation. *Midwest Studies in Philosophy* 9, 371–384.

Verkuyl, H. 1972. *On the compositional nature of the aspects*. Dordrecht: Reidel.

Verkuyl, H. 1989. Aspectual classes and aspectual composition. *Linguistics and Philosophy* 12,
39–94.

Vet, C., ed. 1985. *La pragmatique des temps verbaux*. Paris: Larousse.

Vlach, F. 1981. The semantics of the progressive. In Tedeschi and Zaenen 1981, 271–292.

Webber, B. 1978. A formal approach to discourse anaphora. Technical Report 3761, Bolt,
Beranek and Newman, Inc., Cambridge, Mass.

Webber, B. 1983. So what can we talk about now? In M. Brady and R. Berwick, eds.,
Computational models of discourse, 331–371. Cambridge, Mass: MIT Press.

Webber, B. 1987. The interpretation of tense in discourse. In *Proceedings of the 25th Annual
Meeting of the Association for Computational Linguistics*, 147–154. Association for
Computational Linguistics.

Webber, B. 1988. Tense as discourse anaphor. *Computational Linguistics* 14.2, 61–73.

Weinreich, H. 1964. *Tempus: Besprochene und erzählte Welt.* (3. Auflage.) Stuttgart: Kohlhammer.

Westerståhl, D. 1990. Parametric types and propositions in first-order situation theory. In R. Cooper, K. Mukai, and J. Perry, eds., *Situation theory and its applications, vol. 1,* 193–230. CSLI Lecture Notes 22, Stanford University. Distributed by University of Chicago Press.

Wiener, N. 1914. A contribution to the theory of relative position. *Proceedings of the Cambridge Philosophical Society* 17, 441–449.

Williams, E. 1977. Discourse and Logical Form. *Linguistic Inquiry* 8, 107–139.

Wittgenstein, L. 1980. *Remarks on the philosophy of psychology , vol. 1.* G. Anscombe and G. von Wright, eds. Oxford: Blackwell.

Wunderlich, D. 1970. *Tempus und Zeitreferenz im Deutschen.* Munich: Hueber.

Index

142   Index

DATE DUE

DEC 1 9 1997			
OCT 0 6 REC'D			
NOV 1 3 1997			
NOV 0 9 1997			